ENDING
THE PURSUIT
OF HAPPINESS

ENDING

THE PURSUIT

OF HAPPINESS

A ZEN GUIDE

BARRY MAGID

WISDOM PUBLICATIONS • BOSTON

Wisdom Publications, Inc.
199 Elm Street
Somerville MA 02144 USA
www.wisdompubs.org

Library of Congress Cataloging-in-Publication Data
Magid, Barry.
  Ending the pursuit of happiness : a Zen guide / Barry Magid.
    p. cm.
  ISBN 0-86171-553-5 (pbk. : alk. paper)
  1. Religious life—Zen Buddhism. 2. Zen Buddhism—Doctrines. I. Title.
  BQ9286.B336 2008
  294.3'444—dc22

                                         2008002691

ISBN 978-0-86171-553-4
eBook ISBN 978-0-86171-976-1

16 15 14 13 12
 5   4   3   2

Cover design by Phil Pascuzzo. Interior design by DC Design. Set in Sabon,
11/16. Calligraphy on page viii by the author.

Wisdom Publications' books are printed on acid-free paper and meet the
guidelines for permanence and durability of the Production Guidelines for
Book Longevity of the Council on Library Resources.

Printed in the United States of America

MIX
Paper
FSC FSC® C011935   This book was produced with environmental mindfulness. We have
elected to print this title on 30% PCW recycled paper. As a result, we have
saved the following resources: 6 trees, 2 million BTUs of energy, 610 lbs. of greenhouse gases,
2,756 gallons of water, and 174 lbs. of solid waste. For more information, please visit our web-
site, www.wisdompubs.org. This paper is also FSC® certified. For more information, please
visit www.fscus.org.

CONTENTS

F IT

AIN'T

BROKE

DON'T

FIX IT

IF IT AIN'T BROKE, DON'T FIX IT.

The title of this introduction—and one of the main themes of this book—isn't taken from some thousand-year-old Zen text, although we can find echoes of it in such Chinese classics as the *Tao Te Ching* or *Hsin Hsin Ming*. But just as the old masters spoke in the colloquial language of their time, so we need to find our own contemporary American way of talking about what they transmitted to us. The saying "If it ain't broke, don't fix it" is one of those bits of folk wisdom that everyone thinks they've heard before but whose original source no one can ever quite pin down. I remember hearing it back in 1977 when it was made famous by Bert Lance, a close friend and advisor to President Jimmy Carter. But it was probably an old saying even then. Maybe it really does go all the way back to China. In any case, in its very folksy American way, maybe it conveys a truth deeper than Lance intended. Not only does it caution us not to meddle with things that are already running perfectly smoothly without our help, it challenges us to take a closer look at what we assume is broken and at what we assume needs fixing in our lives. The surprising answer may just turn out to be that nothing whatsoever is broken and that we don't need fixing after all.

Since I am also a psychiatrist and psychoanalyst as well as a Zen teacher, my professional life is all about working with people who say they have problems and who indeed are suffering, often quite visibly and terribly. How can I tell them that there is really nothing wrong with them? And if I were to tell them that, how would I be fulfilling my Buddhist vow to save all beings?

Everyone who comes to therapy or meditation practice feels something is wrong and wants something fixed. That's to be expected. We come seeking a relief of suffering, however we may conceive of that "suffering" and that "relief." Yet Zen (and maybe Bert Lance) is telling us that our search itself may embody the very imbalance we are trying to correct, and that only by leaving everything just as it is can we escape a false dichotomy of problems and solutions that perpetuates the very thing it proposes to fix.

But before we too glibly arrive at that conclusion we will have to investigate thoroughly all the ways we feel that we are broken and be honest about just what kind of fixing, treatment, or salvation we think we need. Each of us is trying to cure ourself in one way or another, but often our hopes go underground and we are never quite clear just what we are seeking or how we imagine we're going to get there. We may say a lot of different things about what we hope to get from meditation, but in the back of our minds there usually lurks the fantasy that something will fix us once and for all. That fix goes by many names, one of which, "enlightenment," can become a way of imagining a life once and for all free of problems. Enlightenment is real, more real than we can imagine, but we will never know what it means as long as we entangle it with all our fantasies and dreams.

In the first chapter of this book, I will explore the ways we can become aware of and more honest about that "secret practice" that we all engage in behind the scenes, so to speak, in our imagination, the practice that we hope will be our fix or our cure.

Knowing how to look for all the subtle ways in which we unconsciously put meditation practice in the service of our personal psychological agenda is where my psychoanalytic training comes in handy. Psychoanalysis is an open-ended inquiry that basically asks us to look at what our mind is doing moment after moment—in a way that really isn't so different from watching our thoughts come and go in meditation. The main difference is that psychoanalysis also asks, "Just where did you get *that* idea?" In an ongoing dialogue with the analyst we look at our personal history of hope and dread, how when we were growing up we learned what to expect, for better or worse, from our loved ones and from life in general. We remember together what it was like to look to our parents for love and what as children we imagined we had to do—or not do—to earn or keep that love. As the analytic relationship develops over time, we look at that relationship itself to see the ways it, like all of our relationships, is continually being shaped by those old longings and expectations. Are we finally getting the attention we always wanted but never could get from our parents? Or is the analyst just the latest in a long string of people who never "get it" and leave us feeling chronically misunderstood?

The permutations of hope and dread are literally endless and will play themselves out in a variety of different scenarios over the course of many years. What gradually emerges is a clearer picture of who we think we are and how we feel about being that person, how comfortable we are in our own skin: with our emotions, our bodies, our sexuality, and with other people.

Inevitably, there is much about ourselves we don't like and want to change. There are also broad areas of our mental and emotional life we don't want to examine at all and whose existence we would prefer to deny entirely. These are the areas where we feel most vulnerable, most fragile—perhaps most damaged—or those things we are most ashamed of. But the longer we practice paying attention and being honest with ourselves and with the analyst, the harder it becomes to ignore these warded-off aspects of ourselves. The question then becomes this: What is supposed to happen to those parts of ourselves that we don't like, the ones that seem to be the cause of our pain? Will therapy make them go away once and for all? What about spiritual practice? Can meditation turn us into another kind of person altogether, a kinder, more compassionate, more spiritual person?

Both psychoanalysis and meditation can bring about profound changes in our lives but they each do it in ways that we don't expect. The changes that we notice after years of analysis or practice may not be anything like what we anticipated when we first started out. In a deep sense, they both change us by teaching us to leave everything just as it is—but leaving everything alone isn't what we usually want or expect. There are many kinds of therapy and spiritual practices out there that promise to fulfill all our fantasies of self-improvement, if not perfection. I like to say that the difference between psychoanalysis and that kind of psychotherapy is that psychoanalysis doesn't *help* anybody. All those helpers, and those they purport to help, are all too sure what's wrong and what's going to make it right. Psychoanalysis and Zen, each in its own way, both call that kind of certainty into doubt.

If at some fundamental level we don't need fixing, then the life we're already leading, this ordinary day-to-day life of ours, is not the problem but, somehow, already the solution we're looking for. In that case, our everyday definitions of "problems" and "solutions" will have to undergo drastic revision. A venerable Zen verse, the *Sandokai* ("The Identity of Relative and Absolute"), indeed tells us that "ordinary life fits the absolute like a box and its lid." The absolute stands for what we usually take to be the opposite of our ordinary life: something that is eternal, perfect, and indivisible into our usual dichotomies of good and bad, perfect and imperfect. The problem is we are deeply conditioned to see the ordinary and the spiritual as polar opposites. And yet, rather than the ordinary and the absolute canceling each other out, we are told they are a perfect fit.

So this book also will be about being ordinary, and how it fits together with what we call the spiritual. Much of what follows will explore what that fit looks like in our everyday life of work, relationships, desire, and difficulty.

Unfortunately, we think we already know all about what it means to be ordinary, and we don't like it one bit. The psychoanalyst Harry Stack Sullivan once remarked that in the end "we are all more human than otherwise." Sounds obvious, but somehow most of us end up preoccupied with being "otherwise." Usually people come to therapy dreading that they are somehow less than simply human; that they were somehow damaged by their life or are in some basic way inadequate. They are plagued by anxieties and often stuck in unhappy relationships that keep them from living the lives they want, tying them up in webs of conflict and inhibition.

Historically, psychotherapy developed along the lines of an analogy with medicine, and emotional problems were thought of like illnesses that the psychotherapist, though only occasionally actually a medical doctor, would undertake to cure. We have grown accustomed to thinking in terms of mental "illnesses," and treating unhappiness as a disease from which we are suffering and of which we need to be cured. While there are undeniably serious conditions like schizophrenia or bipolar illness that may be shown to have some biological or neurochemical basis that we may need to treat with medication like other physical illnesses, it's not so obvious that we can draw a straight line from schizophrenia down through every form of unhappiness, confusion, or interpersonal difficulty with which we struggle.

Are they all really illnesses? Is the whole human race basically ill and in need of treatment? Or are there forms of suffering that we all have to face even after we have somehow gotten a clean bill of mental health? Buddha declared that life, birth, death, and everything in between is suffering. We will explore how that suffering is rooted in the reality of change, particularly the changes that happen to our bodies. How does what we think of as spiritual practice relate to our embodied existence? Can practice help us somehow transcend our bodies and find us a higher realm free of suffering or does practice always keep bringing us down to earth? What do all those sages mean by "enlightenment" and what kind of difference will practice make in our lives?

In my previous book, *Ordinary Mind: Exploring the Common Ground of Zen and Psychoanalysis,* I examined how it's possible to integrate the way psychoanalysis talks about the self, both a person's healthy development and his or her pathological difficulties, with Zen Buddhism's way of talking about *no*-self, the self's essential emptiness, and its interdependent connectedness with all existence. In this book, I will not make any further attempt to define or justify an integrated approach to Zen and psychoanalysis—I will simply illustrate it as I go. The style of this book will therefore be less explicitly psychoanalytic. I hope my experience and expertise as a psychoanalyst, though it necessarily informs everything I write, will, for the most part, remain unobtrusively in the background.

Nonetheless, when we turn to what Zen practice means for our relationships and what it tells us—and doesn't tell us—about sexual passion and spiritual compassion, I will draw more explicitly on my clinical experience.

Ordinary Mind also included formal commentaries on various *koans*. Koan commentary is one of the most traditional forms of Zen teaching, and I wanted to show how such commentaries could be made relevant to a modern psychologically-minded audience. In this book, I will talk about koans more informally and use them simply as the old case examples that they are (*koan* means "public case" in Japanese) in order to illustrate a particular topic. Although the old cases can be used to illuminate a variety of issues, in their most basic form they pose a question whose very form exemplifies or actually heightens the problem it poses. Thus, in the first case students traditionally encounter, a young monk asks his teacher, "Does a dog have buddha-nature or not?" The question reflects our own preoccupation with what we have or don't have, with what's base about ourselves and what we imagine is spiritual. It reveals the basic gap most of us experience between who we think we are and what we want to attain. That way of experiencing life as either/or, and ourselves in terms of *have* or *have not,* is the shape of our most basic conflicts. The koan challenges us not to answer the question, but to radically escape from its (and our own) arbitrary dichotomies.

As an analyst, I know that therapy can help solve problems, but it can also have the unintended consequence of perpetuating a person's idea that there is something basically wrong with him or her, some sort of fundamental, inner psychological damage that will require a lifetime of work to correct—if that is even possible. It doesn't matter whether that "damage" is conceptualized as biologically based or laid down in childhood traumas that are forever and irreducibly etched into who we are "deep down." Too often so-called insights into the nature of our illness or a reconstruction of childhood trauma may simply be a crutch that confirm a belief in our intrinsic infirmity rather than give rise to the strength to trust our own resiliency in the face of our life as it is. Zen offers us a counterbalancing insight into our essential wholeness, a wholeness to which nothing need be added or subtracted—or indeed even could be. We are like water which can't—and doesn't need to—get any wetter.

What then becomes of the "helping professions" or "saving all beings" from suffering? We are surrounded by therapies and diets and self-improvement programs, all of which promise to fix us. What we don't realize is the way all of them tacitly reinforce our assumption that we are broken and need fixing. What if, instead of searching for the latest fix, we really deeply challenged that assumption once and for all? We will need to look where that challenge leads us and explore how it has been differently addressed in different traditions, psychological, philosophical and religious, lay and monastic, Western and Eastern.

By the end, I hope you will see how a new psychologically-minded Zen practice can be relevant to your daily life in twenty-first-century America.

CHAPTER ONE

OUR SECRET PRACTICE

1. WHAT IS MEDITATION?

A great variety of different techniques from many different cultures and traditions all go by the name "meditation." Some call for us to concentrate all our attention on one thing, a single word or mantra, like Mu, for instance. Some advise that we count our breaths from one to ten, over and over. Others suggest that instead of focusing our attention on one thing, we allow our attention to be wide open and simply observe whatever occurs moment after moment. My own teacher, Joko Beck, who herself was trained by a Japanese Zen teacher in America, recommended that students begin with the practice of labeling their thoughts.

As we sit, thoughts inevitably occur; when one arises we simply repeat it silently to ourselves. For example, when we notice ourselves thinking about something from our job, we might say, "thinking: I must get the report in by noon." Whenever a thought arises we simply repeat it, and as we do this over and over, we start to experience thinking as an ongoing process that has its own pace and rhythm. When we notice certain patterns recurring over and over, we might pick a simple one-word label like "work" or "planning" to cover all the little variations on the recurrent theme. As we settle into doing this kind of practice, we don't try to make the thoughts go away or cultivate any particular state, we simply notice and label our thoughts and let our mind settle down—or not—all on its own.

Although the word "meditation" has many spiritual connotations, all we're really doing is sitting there. As we sit, we feel ourselves breathe. There's no need to worry about thoughts, we just sit there and feel ourselves breathe. Nowadays, the literal, physical act of sitting is sometimes taken for granted and the emphasis is placed on what's going on in our minds. But meditation is a physical activity, not just a mental one. We *sit* in a particular posture, traditionally cross-legged, so that our knees are firmly on the ground and our back is straight. We might think of meditation as a form of yoga with a single posture that we stay with for a lifetime. Being able to hold a physical posture is an important correlate to being able to remain mentally focused and concentrated. Staying attuned to our body is our most fundamental discipline of awareness.

However, for Western students of Zen, cross-legged sitting traditionally posed problems of endurance as well as of awareness. Indeed, when I started out, it often seemed that the one thing I was learning to do in the *zendo*, the meditation hall, was to sit absolutely still even though I was in intense pain. The only thing I remember of my first Japanese teacher's words during my first *sesshin* (as the intensive meditation retreats are called in the Zen tradition) was his growling the word "endurance" in the midst of a painfully long sitting period.

He may have had all sorts of interesting things to say on other subjects, but the only thing I could concentrate on was getting from one painful breath to another while my ankles and knees felt like burning needles had been plunged deep inside my joints. Those early years of zazen were physically very painful ones—and I have chosen not to pass this particular legacy on to my own students. Sitting still amid a certain amount of pain or restlessness is a very valuable form of discipline, but the point of Zen practice is not to train people to hold out under torture. Students can sit still and straight in chairs if sitting cross-legged is unbearable and people need to learn for themselves what amount of difficulty is useful for them to bear and why. Traditional Zen had a very macho side to it, one that thankfully has softened over the years, in no small part due to a new generation of American teachers, especially women teachers, who have found new ways to balance discipline with gentleness.

When we enter the zendo for the first time and look at the stillness of the meditators there, we might imagine that they have all reached a state of complete inner stillness as well. Once we sit down ourselves however, we realize that the two do not automatically go together. Instead, the stillness of our bodies gradually creates a container for our agitated thoughts and feelings. They may gradually settle down or they may seethe and churn for a long while. Whatever is going on inside, we simply sit and breathe.

It's really very simple, but it's hard for us to keep it simple, to let it stay simple. We complicate it by being preoccupied with the content of our thoughts rather than simply letting thoughts float through our mind like clouds through the sky. So much of what's involved in meditation instruction is a matter of finding ways to keep it simple. Everyone knows how to breathe; anyone can feel the breath as it fills the chest and moves in and out of the nose. It's like climbing stairs. We all know how to take that first step; what is not so easy is taking one step after another after another, especially since in our practice, the staircase is never-ending and we can't be sure where it leads. Yet at each step, all we ever have to do is take the next step, the next breath.

When I give newcomers meditation instruction, I usually tell them to sit down and face the wall as if they were facing a mirror. I tell them that as they sit, their mind will automatically appear and display itself. When we sit in front of a mirror, our face automatically appears. We can't do it right or wrong; the mirror is doing all the work. When we sit in meditation, right there in front of us is our mind. All we have to do is be willing to look and experience what comes up.

What could be easier? The good news is you can't miss it; it's right there all the time; looking into the mirror your face automatically appears. The bad news is that is not at all what we were looking for when we came to practice. We are not at all happy with the version of ourselves we wake up to every morning—that's often why we've come to practice.

Our discomfort with our mind as it is, is displayed to us by the kinds of thoughts I call "meta-thoughts." These are our thoughts about our thoughts. These take the form of judgments or comments on the whole process. These are the "how am I doing?" or "am I doing this right?" thoughts. When we label our ordinary thoughts about lunch or planning or daydreaming, we simply notice them and let them go, but our meta-thoughts require a slightly different kind of attention, because they can encapsulate all sorts of longings, expectations, and judgments about who we are and why we are practicing. Our meta-thoughts reveal where and how we think we are broken and what are our fantasies of being fixed or cured. These curative fantasies make up the core of what I call our secret practice. Becoming clear about our secret practice is the only path to true practice.

2. WHY ARE WE (REALLY) MEDITATING?

When I ask someone what his or her practice is, I'll usually be told something like "counting my breaths." But what is that person really doing? Whatever method of meditation we adopt, we are inevitably going to try to enlist that practice in the service of one or more of our *curative fantasies*. A curative fantasy is a personal myth that we use to explain what we think is wrong with us and our lives and what we imagine is going to make it all better. Sometimes these fantasies are quite explicit: we're sure we know what's wrong and we're sure we know what we're after. Feeling certain, of course, is no guarantee of being right. As we go along we may have to radically question our definition of what counts as a problem and a solution. Sometimes these fantasies lurk behind the scenes, operating more or less unconsciously, and the teacher and student together must work out a way to bring them out in the open and make their assumptions explicit before they can be challenged. Curative fantasies take many forms, and when you know where to look, they can be seen in all sorts of places.

One classic curative fantasy, one about being cured by love, can be found in Plato. Aristophanes, cast as a character in Plato's *Symposium*, tells a parable about the nature of love in which the ancestors of mankind have been punished by the gods by being literally cut in half, so that we, their descendants, are destined to be searching forever for our missing half. What we call love, Aristophanes says, is the desire and pursuit of that lost wholeness. It seems mankind has been searching forever for some version of that lost wholeness. Buddhism and Plato however seem to offer very different accounts of the loss of that wholeness and the role of desire in its original disruption and possible repair. For Plato, desire and love are what overcomes our experience of separation; they are what glue us back together when we've been torn apart.

Buddhism offers us a vision of a life in which originally nothing is lacking. Desire, on the other hand, always seems to arise from an experience of something missing. Does fulfilling our desires genuinely restore us to wholeness or does it send us on an endless, frustrating quest for what we can never have?

"Dualism" is a word that Buddhists use to describe the experience of being cut off from what's vital in life. Wherever we are, we feel that what we want or need is somewhere else. We may feel isolated and alienated from life, as if a curtain has come down and has separated us from being fully present and engaged with other people and with the life going on all around us. We imagine, in our curative fantasies, what we're missing and at the same time we assign blame for why we don't have it. We can blame ourselves or blame others or blame fate. Sometimes we imagine someone else really has what we are missing and we try to attach ourselves to that person. We can attach ourselves as a lover, as a student, as a disciple or a patient. But as long as we approach people from a feeling of deficiency and longing, we cannot approach them as equals. And by definition, it is only as an equal that we will have what they have.

No matter how much we look outside of ourselves for what's missing, we always will have to come back to the question of what's missing in the first place, and why we think we don't have it. What has stood in our way? Almost always we conclude that there is something wrong with us as we are. That is why we have been unable to achieve what we want or why we haven't been given the love or attention we need. Our curative fantasies always contain within them a corresponding fantasy of what's wrong with us, a private explanation of the way in which we're damaged, deficient, or unworthy. So in looking to overcome our suffering, we have to look at the ways we have come to blame ourselves for suffering in the first place. If we practice Buddhism, we are tempted to blame our desires or our self-centeredness for our suffering—that's what Buddha said we are doing wrong, isn't it?

We imagine: "If only I could get rid of those bad parts of my self, everything would be OK." Or maybe I have to get rid of my "self" entirely! Then "I" get entangled in the paradox of wanting to get rid of "me." "I"? "Me"? My "self"? How many of us are in there, and which side am I on? How did I end up in so many pieces?

The fundamental dualism we face on the cushion is not some metaphysical abstraction, it is the all too down-to-earth experience of a person divided against herself in the pursuit of a curative fantasy. All too often, or perhaps I should say, inevitably, one side of a person takes up arms against another side and enlists practice itself as the weapon of choice. We do this, of course, in very high-minded terms, telling ourselves we want to be spiritual not materialistic, compassionate not self-centered, self-contained instead of needy, calm instead of anxious, and on and on and on. And while these are seemingly worthy goals, our so-called aspiration is a mask our self-hate wears for the world, putting a spiritual face on our inner conflict.

Over and over again, I see students whose secret goal in practice is the extirpation of some hated part of themselves. Sometimes it is their anger, sometimes their sexuality, their emotional vulnerability, their bodies, or sometimes their very minds which are blamed as the source of their suffering. "If only I could just once and for all get rid of:..." Try filling in the blank yourself. This attitude toward practice, if unchallenged, turns students into spiritual (and sometimes literal) anorectics: practice becomes a high-minded way of purging ourselves of aspects of ourselves that we hate. Our hatred for our own physical mortality and imperfection fuels a war against our own bodies, a war in which we strive to turn our bodies into invulnerable machines that can endure anything, or discard them as irrelevant husks that merely clothe some true, inner, idealized self. We go to war against our own minds, trying to cut off emotion or thought altogether as if we could rest once and for all in an untroubled blankness. We want practice to be a kind of mental lobotomy, cutting out everything that scares or shames us, perhaps even cutting out thinking itself.

When I was a young boy going to elementary school, my mother, along with some of the other mothers in the neighborhood, would take turns driving us to school. Four or five rambunctious kids would be squeezed into the car for the ride to school in the morning and home in the afternoon. I was a shy, skinny, bookish kid—what would later be called a nerd—and I often felt bullied by the other, tougher kids. When they teased me or got too wild in the car and wouldn't listen to the mom doing the driving shouting to them to be quiet, I remember simply closing my eyes and making them all disappear. I just blanked them out. That worked well, up to a point—but sometimes if they noticed what I was doing, it just provoked them to try to get a rise out of me, which they inevitably could if they tried hard enough. That memory came back to me the other day when I was trying to sit zazen at home with my son shouting and playing in another room while I tried to meditate. As I sat, I realized I simply wanted to shut everything out, just as I did all those years ago in the back seat of that carpool. My secret practice, at that moment, was a fantasy of imperturbable calm. Now, as then, I knew it wouldn't work for long. My teacher Joko used to hate it when anybody called our long intensive practice periods a "retreat." "What are you retreating from?" she'd ask. Sometimes, the answer is painfully obvious.

It takes a long time to give up on our secret practice, and to accept that we're not sitting here to get away from anything, but that we're here precisely to face all the things we want to avoid. A regular sitting practice makes all those aspects of life, of our body and mind, all the things that we keep ordinarily at arm's length, increasingly unavoidable. It's not what we might have had in mind when we first signed up, but it's what we get.

We may have had the ideal that practice will make us compassionate, and so we end up trying to do away with our self-centeredness or even do away with our desires—but in doing so we set up one part of the self in opposition to another part. We may say we want to dissolve the dualism of subject and object, but it's the dualism of self-hate that we really have to struggle with: one part of ourselves constantly judging another part, one part endlessly needing and trying to destroy another part—and all in the name of compassion and oneness! The real nitty-gritty of practice involves learning to recognize all these subtle forms of self-hate.

How often are we preoccupied in our sitting with judging thoughts? How often does one part of us say to another: "Be Quiet!" How often are we preoccupied with some version or another of the question, "How am I doing?" or "Why is my mind not becoming calm or quiet; why am I still feeling anger or anxiety?" We watch these same preoccupations recycling themselves through our minds, over and over and over. The same handful of thoughts—once we see their repetitive nature, it can get quite boring. Actually, being bored is a big part of practice; we have to get bored with our own preoccupations. We get tired of them, and when that happens, we can start to simply leave them alone. That's what happens to all those judging thoughts: we don't banish them once and for all, we just don't make getting rid of our judgmental side our new project. We see that judging thoughts are just more thoughts and we leave them alone too and eventually we get bored with them and let our attention to move on to other things.

In a way, we allow our life to become much more superficial. We are no longer so preoccupied with our important thoughts and deep feelings that we don't see what's right in front of us. Practice allows us to actually pay attention to all these nice trivial things that are happening around us. We don't have to make our preoccupations go away either, they become just one of many things happening—no longer the only things that count. They are just things hanging around in the corners of our minds; they don't stand in the center of our universe any more.

After all our futile efforts to transform our ordinary minds into idealized, spiritual minds, we discover the fundamental paradox of practice is that leaving everything alone is itself what is ultimately transformative. We're not here to fix or improve ourselves—I like to say practice actually puts an end to self-improvement. But it's very hard to stay with that sense of not needing to do anything, not to turn the zendo into a spiritual gymnasium where we get ourselves mentally in shape. It's hard to really do nothing at all. Over and over, we watch our mind trying to avoid or fix, fix or avoid; to either not look at it or change it. Leaving that mind just as it is the hardest thing to do.

3. THREE STAGES OF PRACTICE

After we've been sitting for some time, we may see that our practice naturally flows through a number of different stages. In the first stage, we are primarily concerned with our private experience of sitting. We might focus on the physical difficulties we have sitting with pain or with the psychological difficulties associated with thoughts that seem to wander and proliferate out of control. Or as we settle into our practice, sitting may become the source of various sorts of pleasure. We might use our sitting to calm or relax our minds, to create a daily oasis of quiet and peace within our hectic lives. Perhaps we may even experience moments of intense joy. There's nothing wrong with any of these feelings, of course. However, when we are starting out, we're experiencing them in the context of an essentially self-centered practice—a practice pre-occupied with the quality or feel of our own moment-to-moment experience. At this stage, we may feel that our secret practice is actually working and that we're beginning to get from practice all the things we came to it to find.

Even when so-called enlightenment experiences give us a moment of light, at this stage, instead of using that light to illuminate our life, we become infatuated with our own brightness;

or perhaps we become like Zen moths, dazzled by and circling around what we imagine to be our own brilliance. Often practice never goes beyond this stage. Even people who have meditated for years and years can settle into a preoccupation with their own meditative accomplishments or secretly continue to use practice in the service of cultivating one inner state or another. Again, there's nothing wrong with that; it's just not the whole story.

We move out of this phase when we start to be less preoccupied with our own condition and into an awareness of how our actions and reactions affect those around us. We begin to allow practice to go against the grain of our secret practice rather than always to collude with it. We learn to focus not so much on how life is treating us, but on how we respond to life. We are attentive to the world around us and take responsibility for it. We start to feel what it means to let ourselves be open to the world rather than always trying to impose our desires onto the world. We realize practice is not simply something that takes place on our cushions, but is manifested in every moment of our lives. How the zendo is run, how newcomers are treated, how we interact with each other outside the zendo, all those mundane things that, in the first stage, we tended to ignore or treat as a means to an end, now become central to our conception of practice. We may even begin to speculate that any "progress" we think we've made is better measured by what our spouse thinks of our behavior at home than whatever special effects we've managed to generate sitting on our cushion.

Whereas in the first stage we are in danger of becoming "Zen moths," circling around the light of our precious inner experience, in this second stage, the danger lies in becoming attached to making everything run—or *appear* to run—

smoothly and properly on the outside. We can become obsessive or precious in the guise of mindfulness. We can become self-consciously aware of our "compassion" or some other attribute of being a "good" Zen student. As soon as we do that, of course, we're back to the first stage, honing our self-image, our self-experience in line with our own particular secret practice. To simultaneously stay attentive to our environment and to those around us, without any trace of self-consciousness about our own condition is the beginning of what ancient Zen Master Dogen called "forgetting the self." Forgetting the self means letting practice open us up to a world of experience outside our secret practice, outside our self-centered gaining ideas. But before we forget the self, we must, as Dogen said, study the self, and become fully aware of all the ins and outs of our habitual self-centeredness.

Finally, we may reach a stage where we are taken far beyond any self-centered notion of what we want, any notion of what's good for us or even what's rational. I say "are taken" rather than "take ourselves" or "go" because I believe we are carried into the true depths of practice only involuntarily. Now, practice is characterized by a deep acceptance or surrender to life as it is. Sometimes this takes the form of coming to terms with sudden tragedy, loss, or illness. Life suddenly demands we give up what we cherish the most. This is the stage where our curative fantasies and secret practices are abandoned as utterly hopeless in the face of reality.

Søren Kierkegaard claimed this is what it meant to be truly religious, as illustrated by Abraham's willingness to sacrifice his son Isaac. It may feel like we have been forced to surrender our most fundamental notions of who we are and what we imagine is crucial to our psychological survival. We face life as it is, and bow to it as our true teacher. True compassion, a life spontaneously and wholeheartedly lived in the service of others, may be forged in this crucible. Yet no transformation is ever total. We would call someone a buddha who lived that way all the time and perhaps the historical Buddha, Shakyamuni, was such an individual—but I know I don't and I know I'm not. For most of us, our self-protective, habitual ways of being in the world inevitably reassert themselves.

Yet even in this stage there is a danger that we can become attached to our own sense of heroic renunciation. This involves the ego making a show of its own sacrifice, and laying the foundation for a new brand of self-centeredness. Extremes of asceticism, or an impulsive desire to become, or become known as, saintly or selfless may be self-centered parodies of the truly religious life.

What does it mean to totally trust in life, to trust our practice? Simply a willingness to let it carry us through all these stages, which it will inevitably do, if only by finally making us face our own death. But it is all too easy to become caught up in the various dead-ends and eddies that accompany each stage. That is where an individual teacher comes in—someone who knows us, and knows the pitfalls of practice, and who can help keep us on our path.

CHAPTER TWO

THE ZEN WAY,
THE PSYCHOANALYTIC WAY

I. ZEN AND PSYCHOANALYSIS

Zen and psychoanalysis are each profound disciplines of self-exploration and transformation, and each has its own complex history, methods, and rituals. Each has its own loyal and accomplished practitioners whose lives have been immeasurably enriched by their respective disciplines and who are sure of their system's underlying truth, having verified it for themselves in their own lives. And yet, precisely because of the depth of those self-validating experiences, each discipline is in danger of imagining itself to be complete unto itself, of possessing unique insights into human nature that are unavailable to anyone who has not undergone their discipline's own particular rigors, and of being in no need of outside input or correction.

But in fact neither discipline has enjoyed unalloyed success. Zen has become increasingly neglected in its countries of origin and the relevance of a traditional monastic discipline, which has preserved and transmitted Zen for centuries, to modern life, East and West, has been seriously questioned. Its transplantation to the West has been marred by repeated sexual and other ethical scandals that have called into question the nature of the enlightenment experience of teachers who have engaged in these forms of misconduct.

Psychoanalysis, though offering rich hermeneutic insights into the nature of the unconscious mind, has had its clinical efficacy repeatedly challenged, first by more clinically measurable, efficient, problem-focused forms of psychotherapy, and most recently by psychopharmacology and research in neurophysiology. More and more psychoanalysts themselves seem to be turning to one form or another of meditation practice, or returning to their Western religious roots in search of a spiritual dimension not addressed by analysis. So both Zen and psychoanalysis, whether they like to admit it or not, could use some outside help.

Having trained and practiced as both a psychoanalyst and a Zen teacher, I have experienced the joys and limitations of each practice in my own life for several decades now. I hope that by now I can speak to my fellow practitioners and explorers on each side of the aisle in a language they can understand about what is happening on the other. In what follows, I will try to briefly outline what I think each discipline can gain from dialogue with the other.

From my perspective as lay Zen teacher in America, I have come to realize that despite the profound transformations that can result from enlightenment experience, these experiences are not cure-alls from which we awaken to live happily ever after. Every insight is partial, requires long years of integration into our lives, and is liable itself to be incorporated into our narcissistic fantasies of specialness or into one or another of our secret practices. Traditional Zen has not always been sufficiently mindful of these pitfalls and students may overly romanticize the ways *kensho*—"seeing the nature of the self"—will change their lives.

Zen does not have all the answers to all the problems of the human condition. Psychoanalysts need not simply defer to Zen's greater wisdom and longer history. Zen needs psychoanalysis as much as psychoanalysis needs Zen. In particular, Zen needs psychoanalysis to keep it emotionally honest. The danger of emotional dishonesty—or I might say ignoring emotional reality—can come from a number of directions, of which I'll mention just two. First, meditation practices that aim at cultivating *samadhi*, or states of clear, thought-free concentration, all too often end up fostering emotional dissociation and avoidance. Thus, rather than engage and work through the manifestations of fear, anxiety, anger, and self-centeredness as they emerge, meditation can create an oasis or bubble of clarity or calm or concentration that simply excludes all the messiness of our everyday emotional reality. Under the illusion that we are cultivating a higher spiritual self we merely end up avoiding what is emotionally painful. I have seen this take place at every level of practice from beginning students to what I had imagined were seasoned teachers.

Secondly, Zen students, especially those who have had some realization, are in grave danger of imagining that they now are somehow "seeing reality directly," just as it is—without acknowledging all the ways that unconscious processes and organizing principles continue to operate, both on a personal and cultural level. Zen practice offers profound insights, but it also may leave behind terrible blind spots, especially where it comes to our emotional life. We may remain oblivious to the ways in which we have used practice in collusion with our personal—and often neurotic—pursuit of autonomy, emotional invulnerability, or an attempted purgation from ourselves of the longings and desires that leave us open to suffering. We may remain oblivious to all the ways that our reality is an idiosyncratically American or Japanese, male or female, reality. There is no surer way to remain unconscious of our personal and cultural blinders than to imagine we have hit upon a technique that has removed them once and for all.

On the other hand, speaking as a psychoanalyst, I'd say psychoanalysis needs Zen to help it understand its true nature. What kind of inquiry or treatment or investigation of the mind is distinctively psychoanalytic? To be true to itself, psychoanalysis must not try to compete with the "hard," research-based sciences. What is unique about psychoanalytic inquiry and the kind of answers it provides does not properly fit into the category of science. Science investigates the sorts of questions that can be answered by finding new facts. These questions take a form like: "Is there life on Mars?" "How old is the earth?" "What are the causes of cancer?" We know what these kinds of questions are asking and we know what an answer would look like.

Psychoanalysis and Zen, however, address an entirely different kind of question. When we ask ourselves a question like "How should I live?" the answer isn't going to come from research. Discovering new facts about the brain will not help us when we try to weigh the competing values of love and family life versus professional commitment, nor will they come in handy when we ask how we should balance personal happiness with social responsibility. No amount of clinical research will clarify for an individual his or her own understanding of the meaning of "happiness" or "freedom" or "justice" or "duty." Seen in this way, the most pressing concerns of our times, such as the problems of social injustice and international conflict, do not look like problems of knowledge at all. Is there really some new fact, either at the level of psychology or biology, that once discovered will make the problem of injustice solvable? The development of empathy and compassion is not reducible to the discovery of new information about ourselves, our brains, or our neurochemistry.

Perhaps most fundamentally, research will not help us when we find ourselves puzzled or unsettled by the question "Who am I?" Paradoxically, science's failure to conceptualize how we will ever build a bridge from the physical, deterministic description of the brain at the level of neurobiology to our subjective experience of consciousness and free will might begin to clue us in to the fact that we may be looking for answers in the wrong places.

There are basic questions science can never properly address or answer because they aren't questions about matters of fact. Such questions can be resolved only by exploring and deconstructing the concepts and categories of thought that are used to formulate them. So I'd suggest that Zen can help psychoanalysis realign itself with philosophy in the open-ended investigation of these kinds of basic questions to which we all must come to our own individual, personal answer. Being told from a scientific perspective what is going on in my brain when I ponder, "Who am I?" will not answer my question. Zen also challenges us to ask what will change if "I" no longer refers to a separate fixed entity we also sometimes call our "self" and that we always define in opposition to some separate "other."

And even though psychoanalysis can be an effective treatment for a wide variety of emotional problems, Zen can also remind psychoanalysts that neither practice is reducible to solving problems.

An anxious young monk once asked the twentieth-century Japanese Zen teacher Kodo Sawaki Roshi if Zen practice could make him confident and fearless like his teacher. Sawaki retorted, "Absolutely not! Zazen is useless!" That "uselessness" is grounded in the realization that fundamentally there is nothing to gain and nothing needs fixing. This realization is what makes Zen a religious practice—not the temples or robes or rituals. This is a strong claim and one that lies at the heart of lay practice, which seeks to maintain and transmit Zen in non-traditional settings, often replacing adherence to formal vows with a psychologically minded focus on the ways self-centeredness or compassion can manifest themselves in our everyday work and relationships. It is the realization of "no gain" that allows us to revere each thing, each person, each moment as ends in themselves, not as means toward some personal goal. The "uselessness" of true practice keeps it at odds with our various "secret practices," which always are covertly trying to assimilate meditation into one or another self-centered project. With a Zen of "no gain," we step outside of our usual realm of questions and answers, problems and solutions, off the endless treadmill of self-improvement and instead experience the completeness of our life as it already is.

Psychoanalysis is similarly grounded in the open-ended, non-goal-oriented experience of our moment-to-moment mind as it is. Americans are addicted to progress and self improvement. The psychoanalytic method, almost as much as traditional Zen practice, goes against the grain of our modern life.

Sometimes, it feels to me as if we psychoanalysts are the Amish of the mental health profession. What we do is deliberately slow. It asks us to sit (or lie) still, to spend long hours immersed in our feelings, to enter into a view of life that is process- rather than goal-oriented. It assumes that each individual's life and happiness is precious beyond any economic measure and is worth our endless care and attention. It will never be cost-efficient. All this may give a psychoanalytic orientation a distinct advantage when it comes to trying to build conceptual bridges to a variety of Buddhist practices, and to Zen in particular. In fact, psychoanalysis, I would suggest, may be the one Western discipline that comes close to being as useless as zazen! In an age devoted to self-help and self-improvement, the "uselessness" of meditation—or analysis— is very difficult to grasp. Zazen is not a technique. It is not a means to an end. It's not a way to become calmer, more confident, or even "enlightened." Indeed, our whole practice can be said to be about putting an end to self-improvement, an end to our usual compulsive pursuit of happiness—or its Zen equivalent, the pursuit of enlightenment. Not that we can't be happy (or enlightened), it's just that we'll get there by a very different route than we once imagined—and it may not look anything like what we expected when we started out.

Both psychoanalysis and Zen are comprehensive systems of meaning and practice that can fall prey to imagining that they have all the answers. What could be better for each than to encounter its cultural counterpart and have to face how it looks in the mirror of the other?

2. WHAT IS THE SELF?

Buddhism and Western psychoanalysis would seem to hold very different conceptions of the nature of the "self." Traditionally, Buddhism has declared that the self is "empty" or even nonexistent. At first glance, it's hard to know what that could mean in Western terms; it's not at all obvious what kind of claim is being made, let alone what grounds there are to agree or disagree with it. We all certainly think and feel that we, as individual persons, exist. At one level, it would literally be talking nonsense for me to claim that I don't exist. After all, if I don't exist who's making the claim? So whatever Buddhism is saying about the nature of the self has to somehow be reconciled with our own subjective experience.

We can get clearer about the Buddhist position if we recall that "empty" in the jargon of Buddhist metaphysics means lacking any fixed, unchanging, inner, or fundamental essence. So having no "self" actually implies only that whatever we take the self to be, it is constantly changing. This seems easier to live with, even though we may not immediately be clear about all the implications of saying that who we are does not include an unchanging inner "me." We will be exploring those implications, and particularly our deeply ingrained resistance to change, in later chapters.

In Western philosophy and psychology, "self" has meant quite a few different things at different times and in different contexts. We can speak of many distinct qualities or experiences that relate to myself, for instance: as the subjective center of experience—as the one who thinks, perceives, observes, or initiates actions. We may intuitively feel that our "self" is deep inside us, but when I'm asked who I am, I typically say things like "I'm a doctor," or "a New Yorker," and so on. In other words, we identify our "self" by all its relations and relationships in the outer world, not just with our inner, private feeling about those relations. All those ways of being my self I can't do alone; who I am is actually defined by the existence of others and my relation to them. Buddhism has traditionally emphasized this aspect of the self using the rather forbidding sounding term "dependent co-origination." Rather than being something internal and private, the self exists at—or really *as*—the ever-changing intersection of a whole universe of events and relations.

We quickly can get into a muddle trying to distinguish what we want to call the "self" from the "person" whose self it is. Is the self the equivalent of an inner organ or capacity that allows or causes us to think, feel, perceive, and so on? Does it make any sense to say that my "self" is thinking something rather than simply saying I am thinking it? Is speaking about our self like speaking about our brain? Is it a part of who we are to which we can attribute a specific function?

Psychoanalysts like Heinz Kohut, who became famous for what he called "self psychology," thought of the self as a structure or capacity of the mind. As such, it can function well or badly, and be intact or suffer damage—although this way of talking is obviously metaphorical. This psychoanalytic self refers to such things as the state of our self-esteem; for instance whether we are easily hurt or offended or whether we can consistently maintain our bearings in the face of life's difficulties. We can also speak of our "self" as who we are in the sense of our personality or character. A person may have a strong sense of himself, be clear about who he is or about what she wants, or always feel anxious, uncertain, and doubtful about her motives and goals. Again, these ways of talking about the self all seem to also be ways of talking about the person. What are we gaining (or getting confused about) when instead of talking about a person, we go on to talk about a person's "self"? David Hume, the eighteenth-century Scottish philosopher, famously said that when he looked for the "self" behind or inside his own consciousness, it was not to be found.

Yet the person David Hume had no trouble going about his business. What would be any different if he had found it? What does it say about the alleged function or role of something if its presence or absence makes no discernable difference? It seems that his "self" in this context actually had no relevance to who he was or how he lived; that its existence (separate or behind or inside the person David Hume) was a fiction promulgated by certain assumptions we have about what *must* (somehow) be inside us that makes us tick.

We use the word "self" in many different ways in different contexts and we may naturally assume that there is some entity "inside" us that corresponds to each use or that shifts its shape or function in different circumstances. We may feel that we have many different versions of the "self"; from the fleeting moment-to-moment experience of consciousness to the enduring set of character traits that persist over a lifetime and that I think of as "me." But what, we may be inclined to ask, is the "real" me, what is my "true" self, who am I "deep down"? But, really, what kind of answer are we looking for when we ask this kind of question?

An interesting analogy to this dilemma was raised by Saint Augustine, who asked, "What really is time? If I am not asked, I know this, but if I am asked, I do not." That would seem to correspond to most people's question about what their "self" *really* is. I owe this example to the early twentieth-century philosopher Ludwig Wittgenstein, who cited Augustine's puzzlement about time as highlighting a very basic problem in philosophy, a problem that also emerges when we imagine that there is something somehow hidden from us about the "true nature" of anything.

Wittgenstein remarked that Augustine acts as if a very deep mystery is hidden in the elusive definition of time. Yet, Wittgenstein asked, what exactly is the problem?

> If I know how to use the word "time," if I understand it in the most diverse contexts, then I know precisely "what time is" and no formulation can make this clearer to me. And should I have to explain the meaning of the word to somebody, I would teach him to use the word in typical cases, i.e., in cases such as "I have no time," "this is not the time for that," "too much time has passed since then," etc. In short, I would lay out the whole complicated grammar of the word, I would, as it were, travel down all the lines that language has prepared for the use of the word—and that would convey to him an understanding of the word "time."

Yet, somehow we are left unsatisfied by this explanation— we might complain that Wittgenstein has explained the *word,* but not the *thing,* namely time itself. But this for Wittgenstein is precisely where we go astray. We come upon certain substantive nouns like "space" or "time" or "truth" or "good" and, as Wittgenstein says:

> We search for formulas which are to enunciate the innermost essence of concepts. One asks, "What are space and

time? What is their essence?" One complains that psychology has not yet unearthed the secret of consciousness. One specifies as the ultimate goal of logic the fathoming of the essence of truth. And so on... A substantive [noun] misleads us into looking for a substance.

Wittgenstein called this "Socrates' Problem," because Plato famously had Socrates ask how we can understand the meaning of the word "good" in all its various contexts (a good man, a good hammer, a good meal, a good life, etc.) unless we understand what "the Good" is in and of itself.

Adding to Wittgenstein's list of misleading substantives, it seems to me that the Buddha was telling us that the most important and misleading of all is the word "self." The Buddha's declaration that the self is "empty" is making exactly Wittgenstein's point about time and truth and "the Good" and so on. Self is a myriad. We can use the word to cover both our sense of extension over time—the feeling that somehow I'm the same person I was as a child—and for the constantly changing ungraspable flow of consciousness. Which is the "true" self? That question, the basis for so many Zen koans, immediately leads us astray.

Instead of fully experiencing ourselves in the very act of asking the question, we imagine there's another more real, truer, more essential self hiding somewhere out of sight that we have to go search for. Not surprisingly, we can never find it. But when a problem remains intractable for so long and so many answers that are proposed are so unsatisfying, one must begin to suspect that the question is either being asked in a way that makes it inherently unanswerable or that we are looking for the wrong kind of answer. We are often looking in the wrong place for what our preconceptions tell us an answer must look like, all the while overlooking a solution that has been hidden in plain sight all along.

"Self" is not a single thing in a thousand guises; it is a word for the thousand guises themselves. To understand the "self" is to understand the usage of the word within the full range of its seeming contradictory manifestations. Now it's this, now it's that. Only when we try to grasp an essence or assert the priority of one aspect of self-experience over another do we find ourselves entangled in philosophical brambles with very real emotional thorns. Wittgenstein repeatedly said that the job of philosophy is not to answer questions like these, but to *dissolve* them, to show that they are nothing but pseudo-problems thrown up by particular aspects of our language. In taking this approach to what had traditionally been seen as intractable metaphysical conundrums, Wittgenstein, I believe, comes the closest of any Western philosopher to Zen. As is the case when we "solve" a koan, it's not that we now have an answer; rather the whole framework in which we have posed the question has been dissolved.

So: How can we train ourselves not to be misled by the problems—or are they the pseudo-problems?—of life? That is literally the work of a lifetime, a lifetime of practice. The form of that practice may differ in different times and places; now it will be called philosophy, another time meditation, yet another, psychoanalysis. Whatever form it takes, practice is a call to pay attention to who we think we are, what kind of questions we are asking, what form we expect an answer to take, and what are our curative fantasies of what will happen once we find the answer.

3. PSYCHOLOGICALLY-MINDED ZEN

After a century of tentative beginnings, false starts, and slow maturation, our generation has finally witnessed Buddhism firmly established in the West. Whereas a few decades ago, Zen teachers were a rarity, there are now so many Americans who have formally received Dharma transmission that it is hard to keep track of them all. James Ishmael Ford, who has attempted to chronicle the development of Zen in America, entitled his history *Zen Master Who?*, reflecting the bewildering array of new names, faces, and lineages. Philip Kapleau's *Three Pillars of Zen*, originally published in 1965, introduced Zen to a new generation. Thirty-five years later, Bodhin Kjolhede, Kapleau's Dharma heir and the Abbot of the Rochester Zen Center, which Kapleau founded, has reflected on how Zen has developed since his teacher published that pioneering work. He believes that one of the most significant developments to occur during this period of transition has been the way lay practice, the practice of ordinary people practicing in the midst of their ordinary lives, has become the dominant form of American Zen practice. As alluded to in the previous section, the history of Zen Buddhism over the past two millennia has been, with a few notable exceptions, the history of monks and monastic practice. While there are now vibrant monastic communities firmly established here in America, the history of Zen has gradually, subtly, but inexorably, shifted out of the monastery and into the daily life of lay practice. Lay practice—the practice of those of us who do not reside in monastic or residential communities and who have not been ordained as priests or who do not live the life of monks—is constantly evolving, finding new forms of expression and levels of commitment.

T.S. Eliot said, "Tradition cannot be inherited, and if you want it, you must obtain it by great labour." We are not the passive recipients of the transmission of Buddhism to the West. We recreate it as a living tradition in our lives both by our efforts and by our choices. Eliot's fellow poet, Ezra Pound, also speaking of our relationship to tradition, insisted our job is to "make it new." When we read about how Zen has traditionally been practiced over the centuries in China and Japan, or even when we think about how the previous generation of teachers were trained, we must decide how much we can simply follow in their footsteps and where we need to branch off onto our own path. How much of Asian culture must we learn and assimilate in order to maintain a genuine connection to our spiritual ancestors? We place primary importance on a student's achieving genuine realization, yet how many American Zen teachers would be comfortable training a new generation of students who had never heard of Bodhidharma?

We likewise have to ask ourselves how much we view the particular rigors of traditional monastic training as a means to an end, an end we might conceivably accomplish in different ways, and how much we see the forms of traditional practice as the very life of practice itself, a form of life that we cherish for its own sake. But if we practice from a stance of no gain, and practice is not a means to an end, can we conceive of practice manifesting itself in myriad forms, lay as well as monastic, as multiple and diverse as the lives of its practitioners?

All this points to the other major trend in the Americanization of Zen which might be called "the psychologizing of Zen." When I started my own Zen training, psychotherapy was routinely dismissed by many Zen students and teachers alike as being comparatively superficial in its effects. Working with emotion in practice was considered a watered-down version of the real thing. Over the years, this attitude has changed at a number of levels. Many of the current generation of American Zen teachers are themselves trained in some form of psychotherapy. I recently conducted a survey of members of the American Zen Teachers Association, originally established as a peer group of second-generation teachers (i.e., Americans trained by Asian teachers whether here or abroad), which currently has over a hundred members. Approximately two dozen of these teachers—or nearly one fourth of all American Zen teachers—reported having some training in psychotherapy. Many more responded that they themselves had sought out therapy at some time in their life, both before and after beginning meditation practice, and a significant number report having sought out or continued in psychotherapy after having become teachers themselves.

These teachers are increasingly open to the idea that Zen and psychotherapy can profitably work in tandem. More and more, there is no clear line that can be drawn between what draws some people to practice Zen and what causes others to seek therapy. As one teacher told me, "I see the average Zen student as struggling with issues of maturity, relationships, family-of-origin issues, maladaptive habits, and addictions—the very things that most folks come to therapy to address."

There continue to be differences in how teachers handle these issues. Some, like myself, see Zen practice itself as a way to actively engage and treat these kinds of personal problems. The choice of meditation or therapy as the primary mode of practice can sometimes seem more like a matter of "fit" or self selection rather than based on the nature of the particular problem. *Street Zen*, the biography of Zen teacher Issan Dorsey, tells the story of a drug-addicted drag queen street hustler whose "prognosis" would have seemed very poor indeed to any psychiatrist he might have encountered, but whose life and character was transformed by Zen practice.

Over the years, I have seen numerous, if less dramatic, stories of personal transformation emerge from Zen practice. Although many students use a secret practice to try to evade dealing with emotional issues, others, made aware of such pitfalls, have used their practice to deal with issues of self-esteem, self-assertion, self-control, and their personal relationships, none of which would, on the surface, seem to be purely "spiritual" issues. Traditional Zen training can, without a doubt, elicit and help resolve many personality conflicts that analytically-minded therapists would define and work with under very different conditions. What analysts call "transference"—the revival of long-buried longings, hopes, fears, and expectations from our childhood—will emerge toward teachers and may either be resolved through the present-day interaction with a new trustworthy, idealizable figure, or serve as a basis for the repetition of old traumas, disappointments, and betrayals.

Most often, the working through of these psychological issues would take place tacitly, in the background, never put into words, never made the explicit focus of practice. Thus, when something went awry at this level of the student-teacher relationship, there was no language in which to discuss or resolve the impasse. Teachers typically have had little awareness about the ways they may have contributed to interpersonal impasses and psychological difficulties, too readily attributing any problems solely to the student's unresolved attachments.

When a student's difficulties become too severe, when their frustrations and disappointments rise to an un-ignorable level of clinical symptoms, such as depression or an eating disorder, most teachers rightly acknowledge their inability to address a student's complicated personal or relational issues themselves and will suggest psychotherapy with a therapist outside the community. Some teachers, probably a minority, see their students in therapy themselves, while the majority seem to prefer to maintain a boundary between the two roles. I myself am in the former camp. I find the transference issues that arise between patient and analyst to be no different than those between student and teacher, and my experience with the one has helped me deal with the other. In both cases, one must stay attuned to the idealizations and expectations with which one has been invested, as well as one's own responsibility for fostering or disappointing them. I do not see my role as teacher requiring me to maintain a lofty distance from my students any more than my role as an analyst requires that I maintain a classical Freudian mask of silent neutrality. The roles of both teacher and analyst are evolving in contemporary America to include an ever-increasing degree of emotional availability, responsiveness, and authenticity. As I practice them, the two roles have become—in certain ways—more and more smoothly interchangeable.

This I believe relates to a major evolutionary advance in American Zen that is leading it beyond its traditional Asian roots. One American Zen teacher I interviewed spoke of training with a Japanese teacher. He thought that while his Zen training significantly transformed some aspects of his life, it left other aspects unexamined. He concluded, "one area may be illuminated but other areas remain in the shadow and come out in unconscious ways. I think the Japanese tradition did not have an adequate cultural fit for psychologically-minded Americans and so...helped hide psychological problems."

An American woman teacher who had trained under both male and female Japanese teachers said these traditional teachers had very limited understanding of her psychological issues, but that "their views on that never bothered me, as I didn't see why they should be expected to be wise in every regard. I never consulted them on problems in my relationship, or suchlike—why would I expect them to be wise about that?" When a personal crisis arose in her own life, well after she herself had become a teacher, she gratefully turned to a trusted therapist as her guide that emotionally wrenching experience.

In my own life, Zen and psychoanalysis have been practiced in tandem now for thirty years. Each continues to challenge, inform, and enrich the perspective of the other. More and more, I believe, American Buddhism, in all its variations, has begun to take for granted its interface with psychology in all its various forms. Teachers as well as students increasingly partake of and depend on both practices in their own lives. We are acknowledging that we are all in the same business of coping with suffering and finding out what it means to be fully human.

4. LEARNING FROM PROBLEMS

Much of Zen's willingness to engage Western psychology has unfortunately been fueled by the need to come to terms with what finally had to be acknowledged was widespread teacher misconduct. James Ishmael Ford's chronicle of Zen in America is remarkable for its honesty about the scandals that have plagued American Zen since its inception, and yet those of us who were around during those formative years know how many more such incidents he could have included had he not chosen to limit his account to just that first generation of teachers. Some of the most prominent first generation of Asian teachers, representing Rinzai, Soto, and Korean lineages, such as Eido Shimano Roshi, Maezumi Roshi, Katagiri Roshi, and Seung Sahn, became sexually involved with their students. Many of their American Dharma successors, most notably Richard Baker of the San Francisco Zen Center, likewise have been embroiled in controversy and scandal. Books such as Michael Downing's *Shoes Outside the Door,* Natalie Goldberg's *The Great Failure,* and Willem van de Wetering's *Afterzen* document the way various individuals and communities have responded to these traumas.

Ford describes the case of Maezumi Roshi this way:

Maezumi Roshi was a skillful teacher, truly a teacher of teachers. He established the White Plum Sangha, which continues as one of the most important of contemporary Western Zen lineages. He also suffered from alcoholism, a disease that eventually killed him, and engaged in several inappropriate sexual relationships with students. These two truths sit closely side by side—and I feel contain all the difficulties and possibilities of our humanity and Zen way.

From a psychoanalytic perspective, what Ford describes as the two aspects of Maezumi's character—the masterful teacher and the abusive alcoholic—sitting side by side, is a description of a textbook illustration of "dissociation." Dissociation is a defensive emotional process in which unacceptable or painful feelings are kept emotionally compartmentalized. Though at different times we are conscious of both aspects of ourselves, we keep them separate so as not to experience their inherent contradiction—which in Maezumi's case would be summed up by the question, "if I'm a teacher how can I also be behaving this way toward my students?" Philip Bromberg, a contemporary expert on treating the symptoms of dissociation, has stated simply that the goal of the therapy is to replace dissociation with conflict. That is, the person must cease to compartmentalize; all his various self-states must remain in awareness and the tensions between them be acknowledged and worked through.

Clearly no equivalent process took place within the formal Zen practice of teachers with difficulties like those of Maezumi Roshi. Many teachers I have interviewed expressed the belief that it was incomplete, inadequate, or inauthentic training that was the cause of such lapses. I have often heard it said by traditionally minded teachers that such transgressing teachers simply didn't spend enough time in the monastery. Yet, the inescapable fact remains that it was often teachers with the most impeccable credentials and long years of monastic training that exhibited these psychological and ethical problems. It has become clear to many members of my generation of American teachers that many serious psychological problems can be bypassed (though not resolved) by traditional training.

Because of this, my own teacher, Joko Beck, who herself was the Dharma heir of Maezumi Roshi, became disillusioned with the traditional form of koan study of which Maezumi was a master and which formed the basis of her own training. Clearly, she concluded, koan study had not done anything to resolve her teacher's psychological and addictive issues. This experience led her to be one of the pioneers in integrating Zen with psychological awareness. That integration was part of what she passed on in her training to me and what I hope is continually on display in this book and in my own teaching.

John Welwood has used the term "spiritual bypassing" to describe how it was possible for individuals to have profound insights into the emptiness and oneness of existence while continuing to operate in their everyday life from ingrained, dualistic habits. There are a number of factors at work in this defensive bypassing. One is that it turns out we don't have to work through emotional problems in order to have a *kensho* (or enlightenment) experience. The psychologist Jack Engler famously said you have to be somebody before you can be nobody, but the fact is a very compromised, defensive, and dissociated self seems to be all it takes. What's worse, once you've had one of those *kensho* experiences, the inevitable tendency is to conclude that working through all those painful and messy psychological problems isn't necessary after all.

A *kensho* experience—even a short-lived feeling of the essential wholeness, the essential perfection of life as it is—is enormously self-validating and self-justifying: "Whatever got me to this point must be true practice; anything I didn't have to deal with to experience it must be irrelevant and beside the point." This is truly a perversion of "It ain't broke, don't fix it." "I've had a momentary feeling of not being broken, so from now on I won't bother to fix anything I've done wrong." *Kensho itself can collude with denial and dissociation.* That is the dirty secret of Zen. Jack Kornfield, in *After the Ecstasy, the Laundry,* offers interviews with a variety of teachers who acknowledged how deep insight could still be followed by shallow behavior.

One American Zen teacher I interviewed told me:

I think very few people have a clue about how to integrate such experiences into their lives, and that is one of the beauties for me of the Dharma and of Zen practice, that it does that, it offers a context of meaning and guidance for digesting realizations into nourishing food for life. Even in Zen, quite a few people isolate their realization into a kind of bubble, where it can shine only a little light and is generally clung to and squished—the bubble popped, the life spilled out, only a shadow and a fragrance left, along with some fixed ideas about its iconic importance.

The disturbing reality is that Zen not only doesn't deal with certain psychological issues, but may actually create or exacerbate them. This may happen both on the level of immediate experience and on the level of ongoing training. Traditional Zen training, and monastic training in particular, may actually foster repressive and dissociative defenses. What I called "our secret practice" in the first chapter—the way we can make practice collude with our personal defenses and curative fantasies—may actually be promoted or affirmed as true practice itself. That is, practice in all its forms, on and off the cushion, becomes a way of not only suppressing individuality in the name of overcoming egotism, but of denying or suppressing sexual feelings in the name of extinguishing desire, and similarly denying or repressing anger in the name of compassion.

In Japan, I'm told, there is a saying that the nail that sticks up gets hammered down. It's a theme that has, for both better and worse, been imported into Zen training. That cultural tendency to suppress difference in the service of social harmony may all too easily become a formula for repression. One person's (or one culture's) harmony may be another's conformity.

Monastery living, less formal communal training, and, to a lesser extent, the intensive group experience of *sesshin*, whether over a few days or a week, all can provide valuable lessons in allowing the forms of daily practice to wear down our self-centered likes and dislikes. But sometimes, and perhaps too often, what gets worn down isn't just neurotic self-centeredness, but genuine individuality and true feeling. Compliance masquerades as no-self.

As a Zen teacher who is also known as psychoanalyst, I have often been sought out professionally by students and former monastics for whom this process has gone awry. My job is to help these individuals learn how to stop being "good" Zen students. Their lives and their practice has often reached a breaking point and the tension between their idealized Zen persona and their emotional reality has become unsustainable. Sometimes it may take the form of an addictive or sexual obsession they can no longer hide or control. Sometimes it will take the form of an eating disorder or a chronic depression. Only rarely in such cases can their teacher see how practice itself has fueled the problem.

Sometimes the teacher encourages therapy as a way to remove the symptom, which is seen as an obstacle to (but not the byproduct of) practice. Sometimes, the teacher acknowledges that practice isn't working for the student, but unfortunately may attribute this to a lack of true vocation or commitment on the part of the student. The problem gets defined as an unresolved form of attachment. If the student is unwilling or unable to submit to even more of the same practice that has gotten him into trouble, therapy may be suggested as a way to ease the transition out of the community where the difficulties have become a problem—as well as a poor advertisement for the supposed benefits of that center or the wisdom of the teacher.

By and large, there continues to exist within the overall Zen community an idealized picture of monastic practice. There is rarely any acknowledgment that the particular forms of that training may, for many, be part of the problem, not part of the solution. It is particularly hard to come to terms with the possibility that some teachers themselves have had their emotional lives badly warped by their traditional training.

The Catholic Church has, in recent years, been forced to look at the way the ideal of a celibate priesthood has placed an unrealistic, unsustainable emotional demand on a significant number of its clergy. It has become a commonplace sentiment, to the point of satire and ribald humor, that the priesthood is hardly the place to develop a healthy acceptance of one's sexuality. Sexual misconduct has led to more and more questions being asked about the nature of priestly formation. Some bemoan the number of covertly homosexual clergymen, usually with the assumption that the solution is to weed out homosexuals, instead of the more obvious alternative of stoping forcing them to deny or suppress their sexual orientation. Something that to contemporary psychologically-minded Americans looks emotionally unrealistic and something that looks deeply fearful—and especially homophobic—has long been ingrained in Catholic doctrine and practice.

Because of a variety of historical circumstances peculiar to Zen's historico-cultural development in Meiji-era Japan, Zen clergy in Japanese lineages today are generally not celibate. Nonetheless, Zen may have to come to terms with its own blind spots when it comes to how emotion in general and sexuality in particular has been shaped by its traditional training methods.

In the Soto Zen sect, by far the largest in Japan, married priests are part of an extensive temple system whereby the temple is passed down from father to son. The sons typically undergo three years of training in one of the large training monasteries like Eiheiji, but after they return home, their duties center around their ceremonial responsibilities to their neighborhood parish—and meditation plays a very minor part in their lives. Only a small minority continues the practice of zazen.

This situation is in part what led the first generation of Japanese teachers to seek out American students who were actually interested in learning to meditate, and cultivating it as a lifelong practice. In America today, many, if not, most Zen teachers do their best to balance family life with their teaching responsibilities. Only a small percentage of teachers are financially fully supported by their students. Some rely on their spouse's or partner's incomes and most continue to support themselves with a regular day job. Although I have no statistics to back it up, my personal impression is that the marriages of American Zen teachers are no more stable than those in the population at large (and I doubt that psychoanalysts fare any better in this regard). Although we would like to imagine that a lifetime of practice brings with it a range of interpersonal skills, it is also evidently the case that a teacher's life also brings with it a range of stressful responsibilities, divided loyalties, and all the temptations of being idealized by one's students.

We are going to have to get over being shocked that teachers are human. It will be easier when the teachers routinely admit this fact too, especially to themselves.

It is not yet clear how Zen in America will become emotionally as well as spiritually mature. I do not believe it will come about by somehow transplanting a more "authentic" (by which one might read "authentically Japanese") training monastery into this country and thereby forging a next generation of stronger and more ethical teachers. Rather than recreating and reforming monastic training programs in America, a psychologically-minded lay practice may just turn out to be the corrective that traditional Zen needs. Only time will tell.

CHAPTER THREE

ORDINARY LIFE

I. YOUR ORDINARY MIND IS THE WAY

When Zen Master Joshu (in Chinese, Chao-chou) was a young monk he asked his teacher Nansen (or Nan-ch'üan), "What is the Way?" His teacher replied, "Your ordinary mind is the Way." By "ordinary," Nansen meant the mind Joshu already had; he didn't need to turn it, or himself, into something else. He didn't need to put, as the Zen saying goes, another head on top of the one he already had. Unfortunately, these days when we hear the word ordinary, we are inclined to think it means "average or typical" or even "mediocre." We contrast ordinary with special, and decide, given the choice, we'd rather be special. But our practice won't make us special; it will keep bringing us back to who we already are. Nansen's message to Joshu ought to be good news—who you already are is exactly what you've been looking for—but for most of us it feels like anything but. We go into therapy or Zen practice precisely because we don't like all sorts of things about the mind we've got, and

43

we're more than eager to sign up for anything that holds out the prospect of being able to trade it in for a newer, shinier model.

The tension between ordinary mind as the Way and ordinary mind as the problem forms the crux of our practice. None of us want to accept the mind that we have got. We come to practice because there are aspects of our mind that we don't know how to comes to terms with. Everybody will have a different version of what those parts are. For some, it is anger, for others, it is their sexuality or their anxiety. It can be anything we haven't come to terms with in our lives. But, in our sitting, we find out that we have to face exactly those things that we don't want to face. Joko used to say that it usually took several years for people to see what practice was really about, and then most of them would quit. They would go off and find some way of pursuing their idealized fantasy of the spiritual life, rather than admit that practice inevitably means sitting with our ordinary mind.

Sometimes when I talk about ordinary mind, people give me a funny look and then say something like, "You're the least ordinary guy I know." I could defend myself against that charge by countering that I live a middle-class life that's fairly typical for a New York City psychoanalyst—not that that is a very typical profession these days. But I must admit I do have my idiosyncrasies that probably don't make me a very typical American male. I don't own a car or play any sports. I've never eaten at McDonald's. For fun, I've studied classical Greek. (And then there is that Zen thing I do....) So my friends have a point. I am a rather unusual person in all sorts of ways, and (at the risk of sounding immodest) a uniquely talented and accomplished person in some of them. Talking about my own ordinary mind as the Way doesn't mean I think of myself as an Average Joe, though it does serve as a brake on my narcissism when I start thinking I'm special. In fact, it has meant learning to be who I already am, but in the service of others and of a life of practice, not in the service of becoming more and more special for the sake of my own ego.

For most people, just the thought of being ordinary is a like a cross to a vampire; it's the thing they fear the most. We want to be unique and special, not ordinary, and we turn to books on Zen, perhaps, to help turn us into the kind of special person we want to be.

The dread of being ordinary has many roots deep in our psychological makeup. We may dread being lost in the crowd, feeling that we have never gotten the attention or acknowledgment that we deserve. We may dread most of all what everyone has in common: that we are mortal and that we are going to die.

So much of our life is spent running away from the ordinary, and toward what we think of as some sort of spiritual alternative. But again, return to that line from the *Sandokai*: "ordinary life fits the absolute like a box and its lid." That is, there is not only no conflict between our ordinary life and the spiritual life, but the two go hand-in-hand. What we think we must go looking for in some exotic place or practice is actually to be found right where we already are. It is hidden in plain sight. As the *Sandokai* goes on to say, "If you do not see the Way, you do not see it even as you walk on it."

In succeeding chapters we will explore in more detail what it means to walk the Way of ordinary life. But in order to do so we must also explore what keeps us from recognizing it as the Way. We have to explore what it is we fear about our ordinary minds, our ordinary bodies, and our ordinary lives. We will look at the way Zen practice can engage the problem of our fear of our own ordinariness and how it can bring us back to ourselves and reconcile us with who and what we are. We may fear that coming to terms with being ordinary will mean a life of resignation, of giving up once and for all our hopes and dreams and ambitions. And yet when all those hopes and dreams are driven by fear or self-hate and a desperate need to be something we are not, they will only bring suffering, not joy, to our lives.

Zen practice can redeem the ordinariness of our lives and return us to a natural richness, simplicity, and creativity that we have long imagined could only be ours by becoming special, by attaining enlightenment or some other exotic state of consciousness that once and for all will turn us into a wholly different kind of being. Deep down, we don't want to be a human being, because being human means being subject to all the inevitable pain and suffering of being human. Our bodies are subject to change. We can grow and develop, and we can exercise and become strong and fit. But all of us will also eventually grow weak and sick and helpless, some sooner than others, for reasons that may not be under the control of the best of our diets, exercises, or fitness programs. What then? Have we somehow failed? Sadly, many people would rather treat the inevitable consequences of being human as a failure of their project of perfection in one of its many guises than admit that the most basic things about life are not, and never have been, under our control.

2. ORDINARY OR SPECIAL?

"Everyday Zen"…"nothing special"…"ordinary" mind.… When we hear these phrases in a "Zen" context we may often nod and act like we understand and agree with what they signify. But if we're honest with ourselves, in our daily lives we want nothing to do with these kinds of words. "Everyday"? Aren't we always looking forward to the weekend or to vacation or to retirement, always ahead to something else, something different, something better? Who really wants to think of themselves as "nobody special"? Who is really willing to say that their problems are merely "ordinary"?

In the traditional Zen literature, we read of the Absolute and the Relative. Here, the Absolute refers to the experience of no separation between ourselves and this moment just as it is, of no separation and therefore no sense of a separate "self" and instead just the oneness of the whole universe. The Relative refers to our ordinary world of distinctions: good and bad, self and other, special and ordinary. Many forms of traditional meditation practice are initially geared to pushing students to have some experience of the Absolute—which can feel like a very special experience indeed. But Zen has also stressed that that is only the first step, and the student must go on to experience the *identity* of the Absolute and the Relative, the sameness of the special and the ordinary, as paradoxical as that may sound.

One of the ways I've tried to integrate psychoanalytic practice with sitting practice is to explore the origins of our sense of what's ordinary and what's special. For small children, it's the most ordinary thing in the world to feel special and to feel that their parents are special. And it's perfectly ordinary for parents to feel that way about their children. In moments like those, there really is no difference between ordinary and special. But no real-life family seems able to sustain that sort of harmony all the time. Parents inevitably do things that disappoint and disillusion their children. Usually the parents' sense of their child's specialness becomes contingent on the child being a certain way: well-behaved, talented, obedient, whatever. Then, that original identity of specialness and ordinariness may slowly begin to unravel—or it may suddenly and traumatically be disrupted. The child is left hurt and confused about what went wrong. Sometimes the children conclude they are responsible, that something about them is especially bad or damaged. Sometimes they are disillusioned with their once-idealized parents, and they grow up looking for new special people to love or to be loved by.

Having lost that original identity of the ordinary and the special, we typically give up on the ordinary and look to new special experiences to compensate for our loss. Although what we've lost is the most ordinary thing in the world, we go looking for something special to replace it. And thus, by pursuing the special, we are, in effect, forever condemning ourselves to be looking in exactly the wrong place for exactly the wrong thing.

Our practice of zazen actually functions to bring us back to the ordinary and restore the lost identity of the ordinary and the special. Fortunately, Zen practice, with all its old rituals and esoteric literature, can appear special from the outside—and so it lures in all those who are craving specialness. I'm sorry I have to fool people that way, but sometimes the only way to get their attention is to go along, initially, with their projections of specialness onto me as the teacher or Zen as a practice. Once they begin to practice, even if it is for the wrong reasons, the practice of sitting can begin to expose their "secret practices" and begin to reveal the origins of their fantasies and expectations.

Just by sitting in zazen, week after week, year after year, the distinction between the ordinary and the special will begin to blur. Everything will come to us, if we keep sitting and stay emotionally honest. As we sit fully experiencing this moment, experiencing our bodies, our thoughts, our feelings, we sit in wonder even as we sit in the mundane.

After a while, we may no longer be able to tell anymore what's special and what's ordinary. The difference stops making a difference.

3. PSYCHOLOGICAL VERSUS SPIRITUAL INSIGHT

Let's return to the story of Joshu's first encounter with his teacher Nansen. Joshu would go on to become one of the most famous and most quoted of all masters, but in this story, he is a beginning monk, asking his teacher for instruction. "What is the Way?" he asks. Nansen replies, "Your ordinary mind is the Way."

If we think of the Way as something special or lofty, what could be further from it than our ordinary mind? That's the basic paradox we all practice to resolve. Joshu doesn't understand, so he persists, asking, "Should I direct myself toward it or not?" And Nansen answers, "If you try to direct yourself toward it, you betray your practice." The story goes on (and culminates in Joshu's first great kensho), but for now let's stop here and just discuss what was said so far.

If our ordinary mind is the Way, how do we practice? Nansen says if you "direct yourself toward it" you betray your practice. Why is that? Well, because you will have already immediately set up something outside of yourself that you're pursuing, and your practice will be contaminated by this dualism. That's what they used to call riding a donkey looking for a donkey—but this is how Joshu and every one of us initially comes to practice. So our practice of just sitting is designed to bring us back, over and over, to where we already are, rather than helping us get somewhere we imagine we ought to be going. But it can take a long time to recognize that practice is the donkey we've been riding on all along.

When we come into therapy, instead of pursuing some ideal, we may be trying to *escape* some part of ourselves. Our anger. Our depression. Our sexuality. Then we think that analysis must be a kind of mental surgery, cutting out all those disagreeable aspects of our minds and leaving behind only what is calm or compassionate. But neither therapy nor Zen practice works that way. The mind can't escape itself—that would be like riding a donkey fleeing from a donkey. In therapy, we gradually come to the awareness that the mind that's seeking to do the escaping is no other than the mind it wants to escape, a mind of likes and dislikes, of preferences and distinctions. When we try to escape some aspect of our mind, we are perpetuating the very likes and dislikes, the very distinctions and dualisms we say we're trying to eliminate.

When I sit at home, I have to sit amid conditions that are very different from the quiet, structured environment of a zendo. One big difference is that at home I have my dog. He's just a little dog, but he's very affectionate and attached to people and he can't bear to be left out of anything I'm doing. If I try to close the door to my room when I'm sitting, he'll scratch and bark. Louder and louder, demanding attention. So, I let him in. Then he'll spend a few minutes getting used to my sitting motionless on the floor, jumping on me, licking me, trying to get my attention. If I try to get him to stop he just gets more persistent. I've learned, however, that after a few minutes he'll settle down on his own and curl up quietly next to me while I sit. Those first few minutes, though, can be pretty strange. Have you ever tried to sit still while a dog licks your mudra?

Sitting with my dog is a pretty good metaphor for sitting with my mind. I can't make it settle down and I can't keep all sorts of noisy aspects of myself from insisting on coming in. If I fight them and try to keep them out, they only get worse and I'm in a constant struggle with myself.

The only way out of that struggle is to *leave our mind alone*, to fully accept the mind that we have, anger, dualisms, and all. And when we no longer judge ourselves or try to emotionally neuter ourselves, the internal tensions and conflicts gradually begin to quiet down. We might say that this is the most basic psychological insight: I can't escape myself, so I must come to terms with the mind that I have. I call this a "psychological" insight because the basic task of all psychologically-minded practice is re-owning the split-off and denied or dissociated aspects of our mind. Through psychologically-minded practice we learn to accept all the contents of our mind.

It's a little harder for most people to realize that not only is the mind that I'm trying to escape the only mind I have, but that the mind that I'm seeking is also the mind that I already have. The perfection that we're so busy pursuing is to be found nowhere but right here in this very moment, *regardless of its content*. This is the most basic spiritual insight that we can have. *This moment is it!* What we've desperately been seeking is already here. I call this insight "spiritual" precisely because it's not about the content of our minds, but is an experience of delight, peace, safety, or perfection that feels completely independent of the contents of our mind or our life, but instead is an attribute of life itself, just as it is, in whatever form it takes.

All of practice, whether in therapy or in Zen practice, can be said to come down to these two basic insights: (1) There's nothing to escape, and (2) there's nothing to gain. It may seem that these two basic insights, the psychological and the spiritual, are two sides of a single coin. Yet, in my experience, we do not automatically have one when we have the other. No insight is so total, no experience so thoroughly once-and-for-all, that there are not residues of our old fantasies and organizing principles left behind. We may come to a large measure of peace about ourselves in therapy, but be left with vague longings for something more, something we think of as spiritual that is still lacking. We may, through meditation, have an experience of the perfection of this moment and in that moment feel an identity with all of life, but afterward fall back into unconscious patterns of behavior. Putting the two together is the practice of a lifetime.

CHAPTER FOUR

THE SEARCH FOR ENLIGHTENMENT?

I. FLYPAPER

A student asked, "What is enlightenment?"
The teacher said, "Flypaper."

Asked about the meaning of his novels, D.H. Lawrence wrote, "If you try to nail anything down in the novel, either it kills the novel, or the novel gets up and walks away with the nail." The same is true of Zen, yet over the centuries Zen students have persisted in trying to nail down the meaning of Zen. In koan after koan we hear an earnest young monk entreat his master, "What is the Way?" or "What is the meaning of Bodhidharma's coming from the West?" They are looking for something solid, something essential to hold on to, but Zen can't be nailed down. If you think Zen is something lofty and esoteric, the master will give you a shout or slap for an answer. If you think it is abstract, you'll be told it's three pounds of flax or the oak tree in the garden. If you think it is beyond words and abstractions, the master may quote the sutras or a poem by Han Shan. If you think Zen is nothing but our everyday life of eating when hungry and sleeping when tired, you'll be told it's the dance of a stone boy to a tune played on a flute without holes. Or as one old teacher replied when asked about the original permanent truth of Buddhism, "It just changed."

Over and over in our practice we try to nail down what practice is to some technique or some picture of who we think we are and what we are supposed to be. But every picture we have of our path slams shut the gateless gate. Zen can't be nailed down any more than life can be nailed down. For a while, we may get away with our techniques and conceptions and have our practice or our life go the way we want, but eventually life will refuse to stay within any boundaries we try to impose.

However, we can't simply turn off our thoughts and throw away all our mental pictures. A practice that claims to obliterate all conceptualization, either by settling into deep silence or coming out with great shouts, in the long run will probably succeed only in keeping our preconceptions comfortably unconscious. We need to make them explicit and keep them right out there where we can keep an eye on them, not bury them out of sight.

That's why I think it good to keep using words like "Zen," and "enlightenment" and even "Zen master." Words like these serve as mental flypaper for all our expectations and fantasies— so much sticks to them! Beginners are often instructed to sit as if a piece of string were attached to the top of their heads, gently straightening their spines. I like to picture the other end of that string, the part by our skulls, as having a big piece of sticky flypaper attached to it. And every so often we have to take that old piece of flypaper out and give it a good look and see all the mental bugs and dust balls that have gotten stuck to it.

It is remarkable how the meaning of a word like "enlightenment" can change over the years. Initially, it will almost inevitably be a catch-all word for everything we hope to gain from our secret practice. It will refer to that problem-free or transcendental or invulnerable state we hope to attain. Gradually. however, practice itself exposes and defuses all such fantasies we have about "enlightenment." At some point we may find we have shifted our expectations about enlightenment away from some state of ultimate perfection to a state of being expectation-free, we will be enlightened when we see reality directly, and have dropped off all notions of gain. But that too is a picture, a bit of "Zen dust" sticking to our flypaper.

There's an old saying that even gold dust in the eyes can cause blindness. We have to keep going, beyond any thought of clarity.

We will never be entirely clear, free of desire and confusion and all the things that make us human. Enlightenment means abandoning *all* our notions of enlightenment.

2. THAT'S ME

For all of us involved in a spiritual practice, there's an on-going, endlessly unfolding koan about just what the word "enlightenment" means. In the version of the Heart Sutra that we chant, it says, "All buddhas and bodhisattvas practice *prajna paramita* and therefore attain *anuttara samyak sambodhi.*" Both sides of the equation are left untranslated. What are all those buddhas and bodhisattvas actually practicing? What are they attaining?

One answer would be what they are practicing is *just sitting*. What they attain is *just sitting*. But that just shifts the burden of all those untranslated words onto the one word: "just." We each have to sort it out for ourselves—what do we think we're doing? What do we think we're attaining? What do those strange words really mean?

It is said that Shakyamuni, after many years of austere practice, one day simply sat down under a tree and vowed not to get up until he attained enlightenment. What was he after? What are we after? When we sit down on our meditation cushions, what do we think we are sitting down with and what do we think we are going to get up with?

In the traditional story he sat all night until he saw the morning star rise. Looking up and seeing the star, something happened and he is said to have exclaimed, "In this moment, I and all beings together attain buddhahood." Maybe that sounds better in Pali, but personally, I can't imagine anybody exclaiming a sentence like that. But I was reading another version in which upon seeing the star, Buddha simply said, "That's me!" To exclaim "that's me!" perfectly expresses the sudden delight of realizing non-separation. That star is me, everything is me! And like the star, everything is in its own way clear, bright, and perfect.

The capacity to say "that's me" is at the very heart of our practice. Traditional monastic Zen practice employs attention to all details of everyday life as practice in saying "that's me" to everything that we usually think of as outside of ourselves. What Dogen called *Genjokoan*, the actualization of everyday life, was a way of ritualizing each moment of the day, making each moment into a sacrament, from brushing one's teeth to bowing before the altar. There is no division between important and unimportant, sacred or profane; every activity deserves equal attention.

Although this monastic practice aims at being all-inclusive in its attention, what can get neglected is the experience of "that's me" inside as well as outside. Too often, our inner emotional life and our thoughts were, implicitly or explicitly, treated as *obstacles* to attention, rather than being themselves appropriate objects of the same loving attention we lavish on cleaning the toilet. It's a unique feature of contemporary American Zen that a new balance between inner and outer forms of attention is being established. Our willingness to say "that's me" to all aspects of our inner experience, as well as giving meticulous attention to all aspects of our outer experience, is no longer the unspoken byproduct of formal, ritualized practice. Our willingness to face ourselves in our anxiety or our anger in every moment becomes our practice, not something we get out of the way so our real practice can begin. We use not separating ourselves from our inner experience as the paradigm for not separating ourselves from the world. The traditional monastic model worked from exactly the opposite direction, from the outer to the inner. Both ways of course can work—and both can fall short. Working from two directions at once improves the odds of success.

Anger, anxiety, judgment, and expectation are all habitual ways in which we try to set up a boundary and say, "that's *not* me, that's not the way I want life to go." Rather than just trying to jump across that boundary, the first thing we have to do is to pay attention to the boundary itself, the anxiety itself, the anger itself, the desire itself. We have to be able to say to all of it, "That's me." The anxious, defensive attempt at holding ourselves back is itself a mental and physical event that we can fully attend to and experience by letting ourselves settle into its physical manifestation of bodily tension. We practice becoming one with ourselves.

Sometimes that can feel harder than becoming one with a star.

3. YOU'RE PERFECT, AND YOU CAN USE A LITTLE IMPROVEMENT

Typically, during a sesshin, I give a talk based on one of the classic koan collections, the *The Gateless Barrier* or the *Blue Cliff Record*. Although at my zendo we don't practice formal koan study, nonetheless I think it is part of my job to bring out these old koans to help us sharpen and inspire our practice. It's not always easy to see what those old stories are pointing to; sometimes we can bring them alive in our present-day practice, sometimes they lay inert on the page or seem merely to be particularly opaque riddles. At one time, of course, they were nothing of the sort—they are the record of vivid, often life-changing encounters between students and teachers, encounters whose very vividness caused them to be remembered, written down, and studied over the centuries. But there is nothing sacrosanct about these particular stories.

If Zen is going to be a living, not a fossilized, practice, it must inspire generation after generation to take up the old lessons and make them new. Finding the meaning of any koan is not like discovering the answer to a centuries-old riddle; rather, the meaning is in the compassionate use to which a living teacher puts the old story. And not just an old story: real practice, real life-changing encounters between student and teacher are taking place today in America—new stories are being told and handed down.

Zen teacher Michael Wenger of the San Francisco Zen Center has compiled a modern koan collection he calls *33 Fingers*. Whether Zen students a thousand years from now will be repeating the stories he's collected is anybody's guess, but for now, they offer us a collection of sayings and doings of modern masters from a variety of schools, to remind us that Mumon, Unmon, Dogen, and Rinzai are still with us, sometimes wearing robes, sometimes wearing jeans.

Here's one of his modern cases:

> Shunryu Suzuki addressed the assembly, "Each one of you is perfect the way you are and you can use a little improvement."
>
> Commentary: Sometimes a teacher uses a sharp sword, sometimes a kind hug. Here Master Shunryu used both at once. Granting way and denying way. Zap! How can perfection be improved upon, or is it a dead end? Improvement is always running away from where you are. Our teachers were never complacent nor were they flighty. Can you stand to be perfect? Can you stand to be flawed? Where do you turn away?

And in the traditional style of the old koan collections, Wenger added a short verse summing up the lesson:

> The heat of Master Shunryu's heart
> burns away both faith and doubt
> leaving a withered tree
> in the golden wind.

"Each one of you is perfect the way you are and you can use a little improvement." Suzuki Roshi marvelously summed up in one line what the rest of us take whole books trying to say. What he's saying may sound paradoxical unless we see the true relationship between "perfection" and "improvement."

One way of getting at that might be to ask what motive does a buddha have to practice? If everything is perfect just as it is, why sit long, long sesshins, why go through this tough way of practicing? Do we do all that as a means to an end, and if we finally "get" it, then can we ease up? That's how we think if we imagine we have to keep improving in order to someday be perfect. But that's really completely backward. We don't practice to *become* perfect. Practice is the expression of our perfection, which is to say, an expression of who we are. Fully being who we are expresses itself in practice. To continually practice is to be continually aware, to be continually aware is to be aware of our habitual resistance to life-as-it-is. Being human, that resistance never ends once and for all, and our practice never ends once and for all either. Why should it? Do we expect to eat or breathe or sleep once and for all and never have to do it again? "Been there, done that!" Not if we're going to stay alive.

What we have to do is really feel the motivation that arises, not from trying to change ourselves, but from always trying to be ourselves as fully as we can. That motivation doesn't have anything to do with better or worse, faith or doubt. When better and worse, faith and doubt burn away, the verse tells us, we're left with "A withered tree in the golden wind." This is a reference to a famous koan from the *Blue Cliff Record,* where a monk asks Master Unmon, "What happens when all the leaves fall, and the tree is finally bare?" That is, what happens when all attachments drop off, what are we left with? What is the bare tree? Unmon answers, "Golden wind." Not still, calm, motionless air, but *wind,* active, moving *wind.* The free flowing movement of the wind, unimpeded by any leafy obstructions, is the free flow of our functioning, our motivation, our being. Perfect, but not still. Always moving, always improving.

Although Suzuki Roshi founded a vibrant monastic center in America, I believe this saying of his is especially valuable to us as lay practitioners of Zen. As laypersons, it's easy to forget that our form of life and of practice is perfect just as it is. We may be inclined to feel that it is just a watered down version of "real" full-time or monastic practice. We may feel that time for practice has to compete with time for our jobs or our families. But that tension is just what lay practice is and is what gives it its own vibrancy and motivation. We always need to improve, to make more time, devote ourselves more fully to our practice. And we always need to remember that we and our practice, tensions and all, are perfect just as we are.

In our zendo we have a calligraphy by Soen Nakagawa Roshi that reads, "Bamboo/ from each leaf/ pure wind." Unmon gives us a bare, leafless tree in the wind; Soen, a leafy stalk of bamboo, constantly shaking its leaves in the wind. Two different perspectives on perfection: the one, the perfection of realization, the perfection of all the attachments of body and mind dropping off; the other the perfection of everything just as it is, whether it realizes it or not. Lay and monastic offer two more perspectives on the perfection of practice. We are all practicing perfectly—everyone is simply being who they are—how could anyone get it wrong? We all need to make a greater effort, to practice harder, moment after moment, to stay awake, to stay aware, to pay attention.

Wherever you are: feel the wind. Shake your leaves!

4. RINZAI'S "BUJI" ZEN

Suzuki Roshi is considered by many to have been one of the great modern masters of Soto Zen. Sometimes we make or see others make a big distinction between the schools of Zen and act as if the Soto and Rinzai traditions were not only different but somehow opposed to one another. But Dogen, the great founder of Japanese Soto Zen, didn't make those kinds of distinctions and revered the example of Rinzai. Even though some of Rinzai's ways of talking are very particular to his time and place, I think we can still hear him talking about the relationship of practice and realization that we've just heard Suzuki Roshi addressing.

Here's an excerpt of a talk Master Rinzai gave to his monks:

You people say there's practice, there's realization. Make no mistake. If there were something to practice, and something to obtain, it would be nothing but life and death karma. You say, "The six paramitas, and the ten thousand virtuous deeds are all to be practiced." But as far as I can see, they're all karma-producing deeds. Seeking Buddha, seeking the Dharma, is nothing but creating hell-karma. Seeking bodhisattvahood is also creating karma. Chanting sutras and studying the doctrine are also karma-creating deeds. Buddhas and patriarchs are people who refrain from contrivances (buji). Therefore whether they act with or without delusion, or whether they refrain from action, with or without delusion, their karma is pure. There are a bunch of blind monks who stuff their stomachs with food and sit down in zazen. They try to stop the flow of their thoughts and to prevent delusions from arising. They hate noise and seek tranquility. This is the way of heretics. The patriarch said, "If you stop your mind and seek stillness, or if you arouse your mind and observe external conditions, or if you concentrate your mind, you seek internal lucidity, or if you regulate your mind, and go into Samadhi, all these practices create karma." This very you, who right now is listening to my talk—how can you cultivate it, how can you acknowledge it, how can you adorn it? It is not to be cultivated, not to be acknowledged, not to be adorned. If it can be adorned, then everything can be adorned. Make no mistake!

Let's start exploring this in the middle, with the line: "Buddhas and patriarchs are people who refrain from contrivances." The translator's note tells us that "refrain from contrivances" is his attempt at finding an equivalent for the single word "*buji.*" We are told that *buji* itself is a compound word: *bu* meaning "no," and *ji* meaning "thing" or "practice" or "activity." It's a word that Rinzai uses over and over in his talks, but which is evidently very hard to directly translate into English. We can surmise that for Rinzai *buji* carries a very strong and particular sense of doing nothing or nothing to do. I never studied Japanese, but *buji* was one word that I regularly heard from different teachers when I was training. It was used in a very different way from what we find here in Rinzai's talk.

Nowadays, as far as I can tell, *buji* is considered a pejorative, as in do-nothing Zen. It got associated with what Alan Watts called "Beat Zen"—an attitude that some Americans adopted on first being exposed to reading Zen stories. They thought the real message of Zen was that because we all already possess buddha-nature there's nothing to do and nothing to practice. Why endure all that hard sitting? We're already perfect! It became a lazy man's excuse to just read the books, and think they were smarter than those masters who wasted their time sitting.

But for Rinzai, *buji* is a radical insistence that practice cannot be based on any kind of gaining idea whatsoever. He goes through a whole list of things that monks ordinarily think practice is about, whether it's the perfection of character or all the different things one might try to do during zazen: trying to cut off thought, seek tranquility, stop delusion, enter into samadhi. All these different practices, he says, produce karma—which is to say all are just stirring up more dust. All are just one more aspect of cause and effect, of trying to get from here to there.

Rinzai's radical use of *buji* tells us that Zen is no "thing" whatsoever. In his talk, he tries to cut off any notion we may have of what there is to do or what there is to accomplish. He spells out all the traps that his monks are likely to fall into—his way of flushing out their "secret practices." Today, Rinzai is famous for answering questions with a shout or by hitting someone. That's one way of directly expressing *it*. But here he lays it all out very clearly in words, telling us that Zen is not a technique, not a project, not a way of getting or gaining anything at all. In his words we can't "adorn" anything whatsoever—that is, nothing can be improved upon or made more real than it already is. There is nothing to "cultivate" or improve. All our efforts won't make water any wetter.

We shouldn't forget that Rinzai is talking in the context of a very rigorous monastic practice. Rinzai's *buji* Zen is not, by any stretch of the imagination, the *buji* of Beat Zen. These guys were practicing *hard*. And yet, over and over again, he challenges his monks: "What do you think you're doing when you're practicing so hard? If you think you're doing anything at all, you're not really practicing."

Yet it's inevitable that all of us think we're doing *something*. We think we're on some path, and we're going to gain some wisdom. We think that our teacher and our lineage and our way of doing things is the right way. We trust it. We know this is the way to go. All a teacher can do is expose a student's fantasies about what they think they're doing. Over and over, you think *that's* practice? And the teacher points out, over and over, "No. That's not true practice."

What is "true practice"?

We say it's "just sitting," which is what's left over when all our hope, all our projects, all our aspiration have been cut away.

Nowadays, American Zen students tend to think of Rinzai's Zen and Dogen's Soto Zen as being very different. The differences are certainly real. But I hope this talk of Rinzai's confuses some of our certainty about making a clear distinction. Rinzai starts right off by asserting there can be no such thing as separate categories of "practice" and "realization." The identity of practice and realization, that practice is not a means, realization is not an end, is something we now associate with Dogen. But here it is in Rinzai. Rinzai's *buji* takes us very close to Dogen's "just sitting." Whenever we think we have Zen pinned down or neatly categorized, it's our own practice that we have put into a box.

5. IF THIS WAS IT

Although effort, endurance, and perseverance are all necessary components of Zen practice, we should not assume that enlightenment experiences are the direct result of our efforts or will be in some way proportional to the pain or hardship we undergo along the way. While it's true that many people have had breakthroughs in the midst of the rigors of sesshin, I have also known students and teachers alike who reported experiences of deep realization happening more or less spontaneously, sometimes before they ever knew what practice was. Sometimes these spontaneous experiences are what bring people to formal practice in the first place.

We should be aware of the metaphors we use to describe what happens. "Breakthrough" contains a suggestion of force, effort, and smashing a barrier or obstacle. "Awakening" is a gentler word implying getting up after a long sleep rather than knocking down a wall. "Realization" implies a process of understanding or recognition, the way that a face or figure that we at first don't recognize suddenly becomes clear and familiar. Perhaps the Christian idea of Grace, of "an unmerited gift from God," better conveys the aspect of enlightenment which is part of our original nature, and which can miraculously appear any time, anywhere, as the result of a seemingly insignificant sight, sound, or word. What is freely given cannot be taken by force and is as often obscured as discovered by our self-centered efforts.

Or we could say that *kensho* is like taking off tight shoes—we feel an intense, immediate relief that is proportional to the constriction we had put on ourselves. "Great doubt" can be another word for those tight shoes. We are painfully stuck in a contradiction we can't resolve or ignore. When Master Mumon, the compiler of *The Gateless Gate,* speaks of having a red-hot iron ball stuck in your throat that you can neither swallow nor spit out, he's describing this great doubt, this condition of inner conflict about who and what we are that practice has made painfully explicit. We are torn between, on the one hand, our faith in buddha-nature and our longing for an enlightened life (however we conceive of those things) and, on the other, a terrible sense of distance and inadequacy we feel in comparison to those lofty sounding words. The greater our inner torment and the greater our honesty about how pervasive such conflict is in our life, the greater the release we will feel when that painful dualism dissolves. A practice that is endlessly in pursuit of enlightenment implicitly says, "This is *not* it" to life, moment after moment. The mind caught in pursuit, often under the guise of aspiration, continually manifests the dualism it claims to so desperately want to overcome.

Sometimes great doubt cracks open when it's pushed to a breaking point; sometimes it melts away in the secure depths of our sitting. Sometimes it's gone in a flash; sometimes we realize that the questions that tormented us for years are now nowhere to be found.

We should be wary of any picture of realization that turns it into an experience we create by our own effort. Practice should simplify, soften, and open up our minds—not pump them up on spiritual steroids. We are not practicing to induce some special extraordinary state of consciousness in ourselves. It's not something we can make happen. However, sometimes the only way to prove that to ourselves is to try our hardest to make it happen. Only when our best efforts fail, when one answer to our life's koans after another is rejected, will we genuinely let go.

What we are realizing for the first time is what life has been all along. Wisdom and compassion flow from simplicity and clarity; from having nothing to prove and nothing to defend. They are the manifestation of seeing that we are just like everybody else, not that we are wiser, tougher, or in any other way superior to anybody else. They are the attributes of someone who is no longer in flight from ordinary life.

We call sitting without any goal whatsoever "just sitting." But "just sitting" is in danger of becoming a Zen cliché. We pay lip-service to the idea of no gain without actually examining what it would really mean to our lives.

As an exercise, please join me in a little thought experiment. Think back to the last time you sat in meditation. What was that sitting like for you? What do you think went well or badly during that period? What did you like or dislike about how you practiced during that particular half-hour? Now, what if I were to say to you that from now on, for the rest of your life, for however many years of practice you have left—ten, twenty, thirty, or more—every sitting from now on will be exactly like that period of sitting. The same mix of clarity and confusion, comfort and discomfort, feelings of accomplishment or discouragement. Nothing more and nothing less. How would you feel about that? If there were nothing further you would ever accomplish? If you never made any more "progress"? What would be your motivation to keep practicing? We like to say we sit without any gaining ideas, but how about it? How would you really feel if this was it?

CHAPTER FIVE

BODY AND MIND

I. THE FIRST NOBLE TRUTH

The Buddha summed up his teaching in the Four Noble Truths, the first of which is: life is suffering. He could have stopped right there because the next three are simply ways for us to understand and come to terms with the first. The core of our practice and of our life is how we face, understand, and meet the fact of suffering. Suffering is not an optional or controllable or removable part of life; it is intrinsic to what life is all about. But that definitely is not the message any of us have come to hear. So the Buddha didn't just stop with the first truth; he continued and even promised that through understanding the root causes of suffering, suffering could be ended. The promise of the end of suffering is the hook that we grab on to, and for a long time after we've begun to practice we try to maintain our personal fantasy of what exactly that end of suffering is going to look like. But it doesn't end up looking like what we expect—or what we want.

As I've said, my old teacher Joko Beck used to say that it took many, many years for students to finally discover what practice really meant, and when they did, most of them quit. That's because the end of suffering that we realize we can achieve through practice turns out to be an end of *separation from* suffering. Suffering ceases to exist when it is no longer something we experience as impinging on our life, as an unnecessary, avoidable intrusion that we finally learn to exclude from our lives once and for all. Instead, what we realize deeply is that suffering is inseparable from life. I like to describe what happens by saying that suffering doesn't disappear *from* our life, but *into* our life. When we live our life as a whole, there is no longer an aspect that gets singled out as "suffering."

Suffering is inseparable from life in part because life is constantly changing—and because of the laws of entropy, that change is basically always going to mean going downhill. The most fundamental things we can say about existence is that it is impermanent and that it is empty—actually, these are just two ways of saying the same thing. Everything is impermanent because *every* aspect of everything is subject to change; there is no fixed, essential, or permanent part of us or the world; nothing stays the same while everything changes around it. We are not like a rock in the river that is immovable as experience happens to it and around it. The "I" or the "self" is neither an unchanging observer nor the subject of experience. Everything, myself—or if you prefer, my "self"—included, is empty, or lacking an unchanging essence.

The most inescapable evidence of change is our body. Our bodies will inevitably bring us difficulty. Bodies are subject to change, and in the long run, those changes aren't good—sometimes in the short run they're not so good either. We get sick, grow older, and die. There is a temptation to use our practice as a way to evade or try to escape our embodiment—our animal nature.

Most of us really just don't want to be animals. Animals have needs and desires and can feel pain. Zen students, myself included, can spend years trying to somehow transcend all sorts of needs, like sleep, somehow extinguish their desire for love or sex, and become superhuman and impervious to pain. The real problem isn't that this ultimately can't be done (which it can't), but that it can *almost* be done for a quite long time, before we really and truly give up trying. Unfortunately we can and often do twist ourselves into some pretty weird shapes, like human bonsai, that we think demonstrate how we can live in constricted circumstances, under severe mental, physical, and emotional limitations, all in the name of some aesthetic or spiritual ideal.

Being an animal is a risky, painful business, and a lot of people seem to be looking for an alternative. In fact, speaking of bonsai, I think there are a lot of people who'd much rather be plants, if they could. There'd be so many things that are messy about our life that we would finally be able to transcend, if we were just plants instead of animals. It wouldn't hurt so much, and the whole thing would be much purer, and we would literally be able to live on just light and air and a little water. True, there are a few things we'd give up, but plants can also reproduce sexually, so at least we don't have to give *that* up. (Unfortunately, sex in plants involves allowing bees to crawl over your private parts. So it would be a mixed blessing.)

No, one way or another, animals we are and animals we will remain, regardless of our particular curative fantasies and regardless of whatever extremes of asceticism we're willing to put ourselves through in trying to transcend our animal nature. Shakyamuni himself went through a period of severe ascetic practice before he became the Buddha and realized the Middle Way—the way between asceticism and indulgence. Maybe we should just call it the animal way—or the way of suffering.

2. THINKING ABOUT THINKING

People who meditate are often concerned about their wandering thoughts. They are concerned that, despite their best efforts, their minds just keep wandering. Now, the standard answer for a meditation teacher to give in response to this is to simply reaffirm the basics of our practice: the focus on awareness of body and breath, and the meticulous but non-judgmental labeling of thoughts as they arise. And if we have faith in this simple process and practice it on a daily basis, it's true that over time, our minds will quiet down. While there's nothing wrong with this approach, if that's the only way we understand our practice, it will end up simply being a technique for quieting the mind—and, as such, it will necessarily be either one that we are good or not so good at. This is a rather one-sided and ultimately superficial picture of what practice is all about.

What is the alternative? Well, suppose you come into *dokusan* (as private interviews with a Zen teacher are called) and complain about that wandering mind of yours, and I were say, "Well, of course! That's what minds do!" Or, you tell me you can't keep your mind from wandering and I say, "So what? Let it wander!" In other words, what if we stop thinking about practice in terms of any goal or any sort of self-control whatsoever? When we label our thoughts, we're not trying to get them under control, we're simply reminding ourselves that our thoughts are simply that, just thoughts. But not only do we get caught up in the content of our thoughts, even more importantly, we identify with our thoughts; we think we are our thoughts.

In Western philosophy, the traditional line has always been that what makes human beings distinctively human is their capacity for reason, for thought. Thought is taken to be who and what we most essentially are. But this is like asking Thought, "What is the most important part about being human?" and hearing Thought answer (perhaps unsurprisingly), "Thought!"

Now Buddhism has given an altogether different answer to the question of what we essentially are. And Buddhism's answer is "Nothing." There is no essential true, inner nature at all. What is there? Well, everything! Or, we could say, "This moment." And when we say "This moment," we mean everything that is happening both what we normally think of as "inside" and what's happening "outside." You see, the great illusion is that who we are is something that is going on, privately, inside our heads as we sit here—that that inner, subjective experience is the real me.

But if you need an operation and you go to someone and ask "Are you really a surgeon?" what are you asking about? Their inner experience? No. Really being a surgeon is the ability and activity of performing surgery. It's the whole activity, not the inner experience someone has while doing the activity. Who we are when we sit is not something that's going on inside our heads. It's the whole activity of sitting together in the zendo, it's our bodies, the other people in the room, the city where we live and practice, the long tradition that has taught us what we're doing here. One thing that is going on, of course, is that we think as we sit. But it's just one thing—along with physically sitting still, itching, listening, getting up at the sound of the bell, and so on. Thought is just one *dharma,* one event, among many.

So what our thoughts are doing or not doing at any given moment really doesn't make all that much difference. That's one reason we give our attention to ritual and procedure in the zendo. Who we are is *how* we do all these things, not just what we think or feel while we're doing them. When we really break our identification with inner experience as the real me, then the fact that thoughts come and go while we sit is less and less important, less and less a "problem." Let them come, let them go. Let sounds from the street come into your ears; let thoughts come into your mind. Just sit with it all. Just *be* it all.

3. SPIRITUAL VERSUS MATERIAL

Although zazen is often described as a spiritual practice, "spiritual" is not a word I like very much. Too often, "spiritual" is explicitly contrasted with "material" as if it represented another separate (usually higher) order of reality. In the Christian tradition, the spiritual is the realm of the soul, which is believed to have an existence separate from the body, and because the soul is not material, it is not subject to change and death like the body. This idea of a separate non-material soul is regularly conjoined to the idea of a soul that is likewise immortal.

It is a very strange picture when you think about it. The word "spirit" has its root in the Latin verb *spiro* ("I breathe"). The only things that breathe are living bodies. We all have encountered, or will encounter, bodies that have ceased to breathe; that's called death. No one has ever encountered a breath without a body. David Hume, the eighteenth-century Scottish philosopher, dramatically challenged the separate existence of an immortal soul precisely on these grounds:

> Where any two objects are so closely connected that all alterations which we have ever seen in the one, are attended with proportionable alterations in the other; we ought to conclude by all rules of analogy, that, when there are still greater alterations produced in the former, and it is totally dissolved, there follows a total dissolution of the latter.... Judging by the usual analogy of nature, no form can continue when transferred to a condition of life very different from the original one, in which it was placed. Trees perish in the water, fishes in the air, animals in the earth. Even so small a difference as that of climate is often fatal. What reason then to imagine, that an immense alteration, such as is made on the soul by the dissolution of its body and all its organs of thought and sensation, can be effected without the dissolution of the whole? Every thing is in common betwixt soul and body. The organs of the one are all of them the organs of the other. The existence therefore of the one must be dependant on that of the other.

Yet no matter how illogical, humankind has a long history of fantasizing a separate, ethereal inner essence and imagining that, in total contrast to bodies that are all mortal, this disembodied breath or spirit is somehow immortal. It is a fantasy that exists across cultures, even persisting within Buddhism, which would seem, by the law of emptiness, to insist that there is no personal essence that could be immortal. It is hard not to conclude that a universal fear of death gives rise to an equally universal fantasy of some version of spiritual immortality that denies its finality. Hume challenged the Christian belief in the immortality of the soul of his day in terms that apply equally to Asian beliefs in reincarnation. Hume wrote (sounding very much like a Buddhist):

> Nothing in this world is perpetual, every thing however seemingly firm is in continual flux and change, the world itself gives symptoms of frailty and dissolution. How contrary to analogy, therefore, to imagine that one single form, seemingly the frailest of any, and subject to the greatest disorders, is immortal and indissoluble?

The concept of reincarnation and of a soul that survives death and is reborn over and over again was deeply embedded in the culture of India during Buddha's lifetime and remains part of Tibetan culture to this day. The Buddha is said not to have been concerned about questions regarding other lives, only addressing the problem of liberation in this life. Yet folkloric notions of reincarnation continued to attach themselves to Buddhist teachings.

In Zen, that purely folkloric nature is illustrated in a koan called "Hyakujo and the Fox." In that story, the master is confronted by an old man who claims to be a former abbot of the temple who has been reborn five hundred times as a fox because he had once claimed that an enlightened person was no longer subject to karma. *Karma* means "cause and effect," which is another way of describing interconnection and change. Enlightenment is the realization of our being the ongoing product of interconnection and change—it is not the cosmic equivalent of the Monopoly card, "Get Out of Jail Free."

We transcend nothing and nothing lasts, no matter how much we'd like to believe the opposite. As much as we all wish to honor Buddhism's Asian cultural heritage, I don't believe a literal belief in reincarnation will have any role to play in modern American Zen—though we can all continue to enjoy a good story.

A more pernicious corollary to a dualistic picture of a person's two natures is the idea that we become more spiritual by becoming less attached to the physical side of our existence, less attached to our bodies, to the desires, the needs, and the problems of being embodied.

Zazen is, of course, an embodied practice. When we describe what we do, we may put our focus on maintaining attention, or awareness, or experiencing, or even techniques like labeling thoughts. But we should remember that zazen fundamentally doesn't mean just awareness or just experiencing but just *sitting*: sitting Zen.

The awareness of the physicality of sitting can itself take different forms. We can be meticulous about our meditation posture and mindful of how we sit down, stand up, and bow. The rituals of the zendo can serve to keep our attention on how we physically perform each act. We can also pay attention to how our body feels when we sit. We feel our breath in our belly, chest, and nostrils. We may feel pain in our knees and our back. We can feel the body as the physical ground of emotion, as it manifests as tension in many different areas.

When we sit we want to allow all the aspects of the body simply to manifest themselves, and to make themselves available to our spirit, which means to breathe them in and out and to experience them fully. Our thinking, our breathing, and our emotions are all what our bodies are doing, moment after moment. My teacher felt her own traditional Zen training had taught her to treat emotions as an obstacle to practice; in her long career she tried to counterbalance this tendency by making emotion instead the object of practice. Emotion, or its correlates in bodily tension, are not what we *want* to feel while meditating. We all inevitably want meditating to create an oasis of concentration or calmness. We indeed may be able to achieve that—transiently, of course—but we may not realize that by achieving it, we have made our practice one-dimensional.

Joko always talked about sitting as building a bigger container, and what was contained was primarily emotion. She wanted the container of sitting to hold all the painful, messy, inconvenient things that we usually come to practice to get away from. We sit still with what we've come to avoid. Although the pain we may be most immediately aware of is the pain in our knees, everything we avoid is a form of pain, and all are ultimately grounded in the pain of embodied impermanence.

Traditionally, staying with physical pain was the paradigm of non-avoidance. If we practice sitting still with physical pain it is not simply to build up our physical endurance, but to practice non-avoidance. The problem was, it didn't generalize very well to emotional avoidance, and I believe it was Joko Beck's unique contribution to the development of American Zen to bring that part of practice very much into the foreground. She wanted us to be able to sit with the whole range of our emotional life, not just the whole range of physical sensation. She wanted us to be able to sit still with all the feelings that we don't usually want to feel and sit still with. What these are in particular will vary from person to person, and they cover a full spectrum of emotional reactions and conflicts around anger, anxiety, sexuality, shame, dependency, and all the rest.

All this makes working with a psychologically minded teacher all the more important.

Sitting in a rage may not be our usual picture of what is supposed to happen in meditation. But unless we're willing to sit with rage when it comes and be honest about the injury to our vulnerability or fragile self-esteem that may lie behind it, our practice will never make a fundamental difference in the rest of our lives. Sitting with and through all sorts of conditions that don't fit our picture of how we want our life to go may be far more valuable practice than being able to settle into a calm or blissful quiet. One student told me that one of the most valuable sesshins he attended with me was one in which I came down with a terrible cold just as it began. He says he can't remember anything I said during that sesshin but what stayed with him was seeing my willingness to lead sesshin just as I was, cold and all.

When we sit still we're doing two things. First, sitting becomes a container; whatever has happened, we sit still and feel it. The other side of that sitting still is the stillness of nonreactivity. We feel all that anger without doing anything to anybody. The feeling becomes our own responsibility. Instead of our attention being directed, as it usually is, to making somebody else treat us differently, the way we want to be treated, we come back to experiencing what is at stake in being treated this way, what the hurt is really all about, and who we think we are that we can be hurt.

One way or another we come back to the physicality of existence. We're not going to find, in practice, a way to transcend that, or escape it, or create a little oasis from it. It is the teacher's job *not* to collude with people's deep hatred of their bodies and their life just because they call it spirituality.

It is inevitably true that life is suffering. But the reverse is also true: suffering is life. It is in the midst of suffering that we get to exercise so many of the virtues that make us human. Our sense of courage, justice, compassion, wisdom; all these things manifest and operate in and because of the reality of suffering. All those aspects of ourselves that make life meaningful and admirable, not simply pleasurable, arise out of how we handle ourselves in the face of suffering—our own and others'—and how we exercise the virtues or capacities of being fully human.

The Greek philosopher Zeno the Stoic said that happiness is a sign of flourishing in human beings the way flowers are a sign of flourishing in plants. So if we can't quite attain our desire to be a plant in any other way, we can flower in the flowering of our virtues, of our capacities, our wisdom, our compassion. The Greek word *eudaemonia* means both happiness and flourishing—the flourishing of the virtues (courage, wisdom, justice, self-control) is the greatest happiness of which we are capable. They are the flowering of our lives. And those virtues are inextricably bound up with and are defined by life as suffering and suffering as life. They're all part of the same package.

However, we shouldn't forget there's another side to being embodied—and that is physical joy. We can overemphasize the side of embodiment that manifests in painful knees and sore backs and long hours of hard sitting where endurance rather than enjoyment seems to be the traditional virtue. At the zendo where I teach, we have started adding periods of yoga to our sesshin schedule. Yoga provides more than relief from long sitting. It reminds us that there is joy to be found in our physicality, and that we can experience our bodies in terms of their potentials and capacities and not just their limitations.

Zazen—our own yogic posture of upright sitting—should partake of that sense of invigoration and exhilaration at being a body. We need to find the right balance in our practice between coping with what is unavoidably difficult and allowing ourselves to enjoy who and what we are as fully as possible. There is nothing wrong with enjoying our lives or our sitting.

4. SITTING LONG BECOMES TIRING

There's an old story about a monk who wants to know the meaning of practice. It shows that it's not enough to ask a good question; we also have to be able to recognize an answer when we hear one:

> A monk asked Korin, "What is the meaning of the Zen founder's coming from the West?" Korin said, "Sitting long becomes tiring."

All of us come to practice with basic questions we're trying to answer. Perhaps we want to know how we should live our life; perhaps we are trying to understand how to deal with suffering or loss or problems in our relationships. Nowadays, it would be strange for a student to ask, "What is the meaning of the Zen founder's coming from the West?" But with this question, the monk is asking his teacher to show him what we are all asking for, to be shown some fundamental truth we can hold on to. What's the very essence of our practice? It sounds like a lofty question that deserves a lofty answer, but Korin says simply, "Sitting long becomes tiring."

How does that response answer the monk's question? Everyone knows sitting is painful and tiring. He's not telling the monk something the monk doesn't already know. But the monk is still looking for an answer beyond his own simple everyday experience of this moment. When Dogen returned from China, having received Dharma Transmission from his teacher, he was asked what he learned. He replied that he had learned that his eyes are horizontal and his nose vertical. Who doesn't know that? But how many of us recognize that it is the answer to our most basic questions? In *The Blue Cliff Record,* from which this koan is taken, the introduction to this case declares that we must be able to shear through iron and not be afraid to face arrows and swords if we are to be masters of Zen. Yet all that heroic effort comes down to sitting and becoming tired. Even though our sitting may sometimes take us to a place "where not even a needle can penetrate"—a place of total absorption or samadhi—we must still return and face the vicissitudes of everyday life. To borrow another phrase from the ancient introduction to this koan, What do you do when "foaming waves fill the skies"? Or we might ask, "How will you handle yourself when the shit hits the fan?"

In our daily practice, we must discover and express for ourselves the fundamental truth that this mind, this body, this moment is all that we have, is all that there is. We come to practice believing that our minds as they are, our bodies as they are, *are the problem.* Who wants a wandering mind or aching knees, let alone a body that is growing old or has a serious illness? But practice will never teach us to exchange this mind for another one or to substitute this body for someone else's. Nor are we here to *train* our body and mind, to turn them into new, improved versions of what we already have. Maybe your mind will quiet down or your legs will get more flexible, but can your nose become any more vertical? Listen to Korin: this tired old body is not the problem; it's the answer.

5. THREE BUDDHAS

Joshu, whom we first met as a young monk asking his teacher about the Way, years later, as a mature teacher in his own right, taught his students with this saying:

A clay buddha cannot pass through water.
A golden buddha cannot pass through a furnace.
A wooden buddha cannot pass through fire.

With all the latitude available to a modern teacher using an old story to drive home a present-day lesson, I'd like to suggest that Joshu's three buddhas represent three stages of our practice and three perspectives on our mortality.

The clay buddha is very vulnerable. Water, one of the most common things in life, can destroy it, since clay dissolves in water. Perhaps, like most of us, he thinks that because of the way he is made there is something intrinsically wrong with him, a basic flaw he doesn't know how to fix. He comes to practice with a curative fantasy right out of alchemy: maybe practice can change me into something different, something stronger. "If only I could be made out of stone—then nothing could harm me!" Or perhaps he wishes he could be made of gold— something wonderful and rare and precious, totally unlike the humble clay he's made of. The clay buddha is preoccupied with the fact that he is clay; he completely forgets the fact that he is a clay *buddha*. That is, regardless of what he is made of, there is already something intrinsically perfect about him just as he is. We might say that the clay buddha represents our underlying buddha-nature, the natural perfection of our life as it is. Because we are frightened by our own vulnerability, because we are preoccupied with fantasies of somehow transcending or escaping the basic fact of our impermanence, we suffer, feeling only our *clayness,* not our buddhahood. We may have to exhaust all our attempts at transformation, do everything we can think of to make ourselves something other than who we are, before we can stop hating ourselves for being made out of clay.

We all come to practice as clay buddhas. We want to escape something we believe is wrong with who we are, to escape whatever lays us open to suffering. We don't realize that the attempt at escape is itself an engine of our suffering. But gradually our practice may allow us to come to terms with who and what we are, and we may suddenly realize that even clay can make a buddha. We get a glimpse of our true nature and for a moment feel that there is nothing wrong with being made of clay, we're a buddha after all! In that moment we may even think that we have achieved our longed-for goal: we have turned ourselves into a buddha, and not only a buddha, but *a perfect gold buddha!* The gold buddha symbolizes our experience of realization.

When this happens, we may think we've "got it." But Joshu's second lesson lies in wait for us. "A gold buddha cannot pass through a furnace." There is nothing permanent, not even "enlightenment." As soon as we think we have achieved some new, perfect, permanent, and invulnerable state, we have betrayed the very essence of our realization. Only when we fully accepted being made of clay, only when we stopped fleeing impermanence and vulnerability, were we able to experience ourselves as a buddha after all. But now realization becomes something we want to hold on to. Instead of feeling permanently trapped in clay, we now want to be permanently enshrined in gold. But permanence is an illusion in either case. We have to let our gold be melted down.

We have to kill off any notion we have that there is something to attain, something to hold on to, something special we can become once and for all. Enlightenment is not a "thing" we "get" from practice. Anything we think we've gotten—even if it's made of gold—can only get in the way. Only when there is nothing and nobody left to obstruct it will the clear breeze blow freely in every direction.

Even if practice gives us a new sense of freedom, we have not repealed the law of change. Everything, as Shakyamuni Buddha said, is empty of any permanent, immutable essence or existence. So even the gold buddha of realization goes back into the furnace of emptiness. What emerges from that refinery?

Joshu's third saying provides the answer. "A wood buddha does not pass through fire." The wood buddha, like the clay buddha with which we started, is vulnerable to destruction. There is no immunity for any substance. But the wooden buddha knows that wood is a perfectly good material from which to carve a buddha nonetheless. Gone are all curative fantasies, gone are all self-reproaches about the inadequacy of who and what we are.

Be careful what you wish for. Only when our hopes are completely smashed will we be free. It's not the "freedom" we started out looking for at all. When we started out thinking we were clay, we didn't think we'd end up as wood—another material just as vulnerable.

Nonetheless, there is a real difference between the clay buddha and wood buddha. The wood buddha is perfectly balanced between the experience of being made of wood and the experience of being buddha. The two are not in opposition to one another, each is actually an expression of the other. Wood is not imperfect; buddhas are only made out of ordinary materials.

Wood is a perfect material for making a buddha.

Meat is another.

Like clay, gold, and wood, meat is subject to change. Following Joshu we might say, "A meat buddha cannot pass through time." Nothing made from meat will last forever, or even keep its shape for very long. Meat rots and spoils, everything made of meat ages and dies. But that is not an imperfection in the meat, it is the nature of meat, the perfect expression of *meatness*. We truly are buddhas. Meat buddhas.

CHAPTER SIX

LOVE, SEX, AND COMPASSION

I. DESIRE AND SUFFERING

In the previous chapter, we looked at the inescapability of suffering and how suffering is grounded in our human response to change and impermanence. One version of where practice is supposed to lead is an acceptance of impermanence. This is true, but it is only a half-truth, one that can give rise to the fantasy of being so open to change that we will no longer suffer. What we also come to accept through practice is the inescapability of desire. As an old master reminded us, "The red thread of desire is never broken."

Desire is a word with many connotations. In some contexts, it feels more appropriate to translate the Second Noble Truth ("The cause of suffering is desire") using the words *clinging* or *attachment* instead of *desire*, thereby shifting its emphasis toward a resistance to Buddha's fundamental insight that all *dharmas,* including the self, are empty of a fixed, unchanging essential nature. This version of desire focuses on the suffering that arises from the desire that things shouldn't change. We want to have a rock-solid, unchanging relationship to something and particularly to another person. Desire in this sense is whatever attempts to deny the universal fact of impermanence. Since life won't cooperate for very long with our attempts at denial, we inevitably will suffer.

We do have to accept the fact of change. We can come to understand that in many aspects of our life, but I think we face the greatest challenge when it comes to our personal relationships. Don't we have any right to expect constancy from our loved ones?—or is that too unrealistic an expectation? This longing for emotional constancy restores "desire" to its full emotional range, encompassing its everyday meanings of love, sexual attraction, and emotional need. All of these, I maintain, are as inescapably part of the human condition as the fact of change. Realizing that desire is intrinsically part of being human will sharply curtail our transcendent fantasies about ending suffering.

Psychologists (and parents) would, I'm sure, universally agree that an infant requires a basic level of constancy and a sense of secure attachment in order to develop normally. That emotional constancy can take many shapes and there is no one way to be a good parent. The range and styles of adequate caregiving vary enormously. What we mean by developing "normally" has equally many forms, some of which are only now being acknowledged, especially in the areas of gender and sexual identity. Psychoanalytic theory for too long equated normality with heterosexuality and maturity with narrowly defined roles for men and women.

In contemporary Western culture, there also has been an emphasis on the child's need to develop the ability to separate from the mother and function independently without anxiety. In Eastern societies, such as India and Japan, much longer periods of familial dependence are the norm, and embeddedness in the family and society at large are valued more than autonomy. Social conformity may provide the link to a sense of a secure connection to the group as a whole, as well as to one's immediate family.

Whatever form it takes, a need for a certain degree of constancy seems to be part of our emotional makeup. Within the context of practice, this takes the form of wanting to rely both on the practice itself and on the person of the teacher. Each of these in turn can challenge our notions of what counts as secure and reliable.

No matter how much we talk about impermanence we nonetheless all seem to need what feels to us like an unchanging set of values and ideals to keep us steady through the all too often traumatic vicissitudes of a changing world. We need both the constancy of practice itself, and a flexible enough conception of practice to allow it to be maintained under changing circumstances. How we see practice, how we view those background values and ideals that help us cope with change, will themselves be in an ever-evolving dialogue or dance with the world of change. Forms and conceptions of practice evolve in response to the challenges of life. I believe lay practice itself is one such an ongoing response to a changing world. In addition, our present-day practice is in an ongoing dialogue with the past, with our traditions, which, rather than being static or timeless, are themselves continually being renewed and revised by being viewed through different lenses, different translations, from different cultural vantage points throughout history.

Zen demands that we resolve for ourselves the tension between maintaining what is traditional and authentic in its transmission and the need to constantly be adaptive and responsive to a changing world. We need to simultaneously see with our own eyes and look through the eyes of our ancestors.

One question that can arise from Buddhist practice is whether or to what extent will we see the desire for something permanent, or even consistent, as a problem rather than part of the solution, whether such a desire is just another attachment that needs shaking up, if not complete renunciation. Or do we allow our desire for constancy to feel legitimate only to the extent that it is gratified by identification with the traditional forms of practice itself? It is an irony of our practice that we use so many unchanging forms in our quest to understand the basic reality of change.

At the personal level, we all agree it's natural to for children to want a predictable, trustworthy parent in their lives. Is that something we are supposed to outgrow or can we, as adult students of Buddhism, legitimately expect something similar from our teachers? Some traditions ask us to put total trust in the teacher and at the same time give the teacher license to be totally unpredictable. Ideally, that total unpredictability is an object lesson in total freedom. Too often, however, the reality is that unpredictable means simply unreliable and inappropriate. How can we tell when a teacher crosses that line? It's a sad fact that teachers have crossed and do cross it and that we sometimes don't realize it until it has happened.

One thing we learn from years of practice is that the constancy we look for in practice and from our teachers is not necessarily to be found in the person of a unique individual or in any particular unchanging form or structure. The more we are able to see the Dharma in different guises, the more present it will be in our lives. Authentic teachers may look very different from one another and true practice takes many shapes. The more we are able to have our practice manifest ever new configurations, whether in the personal, social, or political arenas, the more reliably present it will be. A practice that depends on one form, one person, one and only one way of "true" practice is liable to become either rigid and inflexible or brittle and easily derailed.

Whatever happens to us we can begin to see both as an opportunity to practice and to expand our previous ideas about the nature of practice to accommodate the new circumstances. Both we and our definition of practice have the opportunity to grow more expansive, more flexible, more responsive to changing conditions as we mature.

One classic expression of this capacity in the Western philosophical tradition is Socrates' assertion that "A good man can't be harmed." Socrates took everything as an opportunity to practice and teach philosophy, right up to and including being put on trial for his life, being unjustly accused, condemned, and finally executed. At every step of the way, he showed how a good man could handle himself under any circumstances. His trust in his practice of philosophy, a basic trust in the value of pursuing and teaching the truth, was unshakable. Ideally, if you're clear in your own practice, in your own honesty and your own responsiveness, whatever happens is an opportunity to practice.

The temptation built into that view is that we turn practice, in whatever tradition we find ourselves, into a project to make us imperturbable. We think that if we're really doing this right, then all the changes that life brings won't get to us. We'll get to a place where we can handle everything. That's another curative fantasy that we have to work our way through. One of the basic lessons from classical Greek tragedy, to set beside the example of Socrates, is that no one is impervious to the will or whim of the gods. Any person, no matter how great, or how wise, or how strong, can be brought low by chance. Oedipus succumbs to hubris imagining that the cleverness that outwitted the Sphinx and her riddle about the ages of man would allow him to master any situation and escape the fate the gods had willed for him.

The wisdom of practice has two faces which, Janus-like, look in opposite directions at the same time. One side shows us that everything everywhere is an opportunity to practice and to express our true nature. The other shows us that practice is another name for being one with our mortality and vulnerability. The first version of wisdom does not exempt us from the second. We must come to allow ourselves to be the mortal and vulnerable and dependent beings that we are. We must see that our practice is not going to enable us to overcome or transcend our nature, but allow us to be more and more open to the pain of being human. We don't have to hate ourselves for our own vulnerability. We don't have to hate ourselves for what life has done to us. We don't have to hate ourselves because hurt or loss or longing has gotten to us, imagining, as Zen students too often do, that they should somehow be "beyond" all those reactions. We can eventually stop using practice in the service of a curative fantasy of being made out of stone, immune to the pain of the world.

Practice doesn't turn us into supermen. It does make us stronger and it does make us more resilient. It does make us less vulnerable in one sense, but it makes us much *more* vulnerable in another. We allow ourselves to be open to the fact that all those we rely on most, our teachers and parents, will get old and will die. When that happens we will feel the loss and have to find a way to go on without them. Our own desires will always be with us in some form, keeping us firmly attached to a world that will hurt us.

We have to find a way to treat our own changing life, our own vulnerability, as we would a dear friend. That is to say, we must come to love ourselves, love our life, in its vulnerability, in its impermanence, not in spite of all its flaws, but because of them. Because the vulnerability, the changes, the flaws make us who we are.

2. ASSES AND HORSES

We are preoccupied, almost all the time, with making one kind of discrimination or another, both inside and outside. We can get endlessly preoccupied with our inner experience, whether we feel good or bad, happy or unhappy. On the outside, we can get completely wrapped up in the idea that our deepest needs can only be met by learning to distinguish what we imagine is the real thing (real love, real teachers, the real *point* of life) from what's not good enough, not the real thing. When we think we've spotted it we say to ourselves: "THIS is the real thing," and "I've got it, you don't," or, "You've got it and I don't." One way or another, we imagine our life and our practice is about going from not having it to having it.

Zen practice can radically undermine that whole way of looking at things. To be a Zen Buddhist is to belong to the least exclusive club in the world, anybody can come in. In an old story, a monk asked Master Joshu, "For a long time I've heard of the stone bridge of Joshu, now that I've come here, I just see a simple wooden bridge." Joshu said: "You just see the wooden bridge, you don't see the stone bridge." The monk said: "Where is the stone bridge?" Joshu said: "It lets asses cross, it lets horses cross."

Anyone can cross the bridge, just as anyone can pass through the gateless barrier—it's wide open. The paradox is that we don't let *ourselves* in. The barrier is the very idea that there is an inside and an outside, that there is somewhere to go and there is something to get. As long as we make that distinction, we don't realize we're *already* inside. We spend our lives with our nose pressed up against an imaginary windowpane, wishing we were on the other side.

Our life already includes everything. Life's answer is an answer of non-discrimination. This monk's question to Joshu, like the other more famous question about the dog's buddha-nature, is framed around a difference, the wooden bridge versus the stone bridge, having something versus not having it, being ordinary versus being special. And Joshu says, the thing you're not seeing is non-discrimination itself, not making any distinction between wood and stone, between horses and asses, dogs and buddha-nature.

When I first read this koan about asses and horses, I was reminded of the parable in the New Testament that says Christ will return to separate the sheep from the goats. The sheep, the ones that God have chosen—or if you prefer, who have chosen God—get to go to heaven, whereas the goats who reject Him go to hell. Even God, it seems, is quick to make distinctions, beginning in the Old Testament with the idea of the Jews as a chosen people. The world is divided into believers and non-believers, those who follow the Commandments and those who don't. It seems we can't ever completely escape the dichotomies even when we have a bridge of universal love. We want to imagine that God's love is indiscriminate, in loving everyone equally, but we have a very hard time staying in that perspective.

In stark contrast to the idea of universal or indiscriminate love is our ordinary sense of love, which is all about the uniqueness of the loved one. In our ordinary psychological version of love the loved one is the most special person in the world to us, whether it's a child or a lover, and we make enormous distinctions between this person and everybody else. As George Bernard Shaw once said, "[romantic] love is the gross exaggeration of the difference between one person and everybody else."

The challenge posed by nondiscrimination is: what would it mean to love everyone? In our usual way of talking about love, it's literally an oxymoron. By definition, love is all about some special person. When we try to universalize it, well, we really don't know what it means to try to do that. Do we really think we are going to extend the same love to every homeless person we encounter on the street that we give to our parents or our child? What could it mean to love a complete stranger? In what way will that love manifest itself? We might think it would be saintly to give away all our money and possessions to the homeless; we rarely think it would be equally saintly to have sex with them. Some versions of love will always have to retain a sense of discrimination.

I think many people get in trouble in life and in practice because they think the real answer must lie on one side of that bridge or another. We think we have to choose between being selfish and selfless, between love that is personal and unique and a love that is spiritual and universal. On one side of that bridge, in our ordinary life, we think that love is what we need, and we organize our life around the lack of love or pursuit of love. Living that way, we get caught up in an ultimately futile pursuit, futile because impermanence will always win in the end. We'll never hold on to the person or the feeling that we so desperately crave. On the other side, instead of a personal, unique love, we try to pursue a universal compassion for all beings indiscriminately. In a moment of realization, we may find that what we need is not in one place, but is everywhere. Rather than having to have one thing, we can have everything. There's an exhilaration in that discovery as powerful and transformative as falling in love. But people can't live on that side of the equation exclusively either, and if people try to live by compassion alone, it often goes terribly awry. Mothers will not end up treating their child exactly the same way they treat all the other children. We're not going to give up having exclusive relationships and lovers; it's a natural part of our lives. When, because of our fears and disappointments in the realm of attachment, we try to live solely in the realm of non-discrimination, pretty soon some sort of hanky-panky will start to break loose somewhere, because the human will want out.

William James famously thought mankind needed to find a moral equivalent of war. Those who pursue a spiritual path sometimes seem to wish that compassion could turn out to be the moral equivalent of passion. Buddhism can often sound as if it wants to replace *passion* with *compassion*. Certainly, the taking of monastic vows, especially a vow of chastity, in Christianity, as well as Buddhism, can be seen as a literal attempt to enact this substitution: in the strictest form, all sexual activity is renounced, and prayer or meditation is enlisted in the service of replacing desire with compassion as the prime interpersonal motivation.

Certainly a life ruled by passion may be amoral and self-centered, but passion is central to our lives and it is very questionable whether self-centered passions can actually be replaced by other-directed compassion. Can compassion genuinely be a satisfying emotional equivalent for the passion that the monk renounces? Or is the whole notion that the solution to desire can still be in some sense "satisfying" part of the problem? It's very easy to get stuck in an either/or answer. It's hard to build a bridge that is wide enough for both passion and compassion to cross side by side. In the next section, we will see how one monk, Thomas Merton, struggled to build it in his own life.

3. THOMAS MERTON IN LOVE

The life of Thomas Merton, the author and Trappist monk, offers an illuminating and cautionary tale about the two sides of love. Merton entered Our Lady of Gethsemani monastery in rural Kentucky in 1941, when he was 27 years old. In 1948, his spiritual autobiography, *The Seven Storey Mountain,* was published to great acclaim, becoming one of the bestselling religious memoirs of all time. Merton continued to write not just about religion and spirituality, but about social justice, peace, and civil rights throughout the rest of his life as a monk. He was one of the earliest pioneers in the creation of a Christian/Buddhist dialogue and was deeply attracted to Zen. His posthumously published journals and correspondence provide a unique record of contemporary monastic formation. He died in 1968 in Bangkok, Thailand, where he was meeting with Buddhist teachers on one of his first trips outside of the monastery. He died by accidentally electrocuting himself touching an electric fan when stepping out of a bathtub.

Merton's monastic order, formally known as The Cistercian Order of the Strict Observance, was known for its rigorous discipline and asceticism. The monks took vows of stability (a vow never to leave the monastery without permission), obedience, and chastity. Silence was not a formal vow, but the norm of daily monastic life. For many years before his final Asian journey, Merton had sought out time for solitary meditation within his monastic community, where communal prayer and the chanting of the daily office were the traditional forms of worship. Merton eventually was granted permission to spend increasing amounts of time alone in a hermitage that was built for him on a hill overlooking the monastery. Paradoxically, the hermitage also created the opportunity for him to receive ever-increasing numbers of visitors for private conversation for extended periods out from under the watchful eyes of his conservative Abbot.

In 1966, Merton developed serious back problems and was admitted to a hospital in Louisville for surgery. Following the operation, he was cared for during his convalescence by a young student nurse named Margie. Although initially reluctant to be drawn into conversation with her, he found himself looking forward to her visits more and more. There was something in her attention that opened up a deep yearning in him that he had never before acknowledged, but which he scrupulously recorded in his private journals as their relationship developed. After Merton's death these private journals were made available to his biographer, John Howard Griffin, whose quotations from them appear below. Although Merton could live alone without being lonely or missing the company of male friends, he wrote that he "did feel a deep emotional need for feminine companionship and affection." Merton, after his surgery, admitted in his journal that the realization that as a monk "I must irrevocably live without it ended up tearing me up more than the operation itself."

When Margie was with him, Merton wrote, "the room was filled with the light of freedom and joy." Once he left the hospital his hermitage provided the means for them to communicate privately and occasionally meet in secret over the next two years. For the rest of his life Merton struggled with how to understand the relationship of that personal joy to the joy he spent his life seeking in God. Because of his vows of chastity and obedience, the two seemed to be in irreconcilable conflict and yet Merton continued to long for a way to experience both. Over and over again, he came up with rationalizations about how "this human love could be integrated into his monastic and priestly vocation," only to have all his resolutions melt away when he saw or spoke to her. He desperately wanted to find a way to spiritualize their love, yet human passion and longing refused to be sublimated into a disembodied abstraction. One side of Merton wished that his love could be chaste and compassionate, but the reality of having a body kept intruding, bringing both anguish and joy.

"We are determined that our love must be spiritual and chaste," Merton wrote in his private journal, "but the longing for her is frightful and of course so is the conflict that goes with it." Despite themselves they go "deeper and deeper in love." At one point Margie challenged him on a point he made about "detachment." "He conceded it was nonsense to talk about detachment when you were in love, and made a frank commitment: he was attached to her and moreover this attachment profoundly changed his life."

Uniting the spiritual and the erotic in poetry is a tradition that goes back at least to the *Song of Songs* in the Old Testament. Integrating the two in real love is far more problematic. Inevitably we struggle to find a balance between those two perspectives, between love in the ordinary sense and in the spiritual, non-discriminating sense, and try to find a way for each to take a place in our lives.

Traditionally, spiritual practice opens us up to the universal and non-exclusive, while psychotherapy helps us tolerate the vulnerability of being exclusively attached to a single person. But the two practices can and should dovetail. In meditation, we can see how much time we spend separating what we love from what we don't. Part of the simple practice that we do, just labeling thoughts as thoughts, is a way of making all thoughts equal. When we do that with one thought after another, we gradually come to be able to do it with one person after another, without all the sorting and comparing that we habitually engage in all the time. Once we can learn to accept each thought, one after another, just as it is, we accept each person, one after each other, just as they are. And that is something that makes living with, and depending upon, that single special individual a much less threatening proposition—we are more and more able to face the unavoidable risk of putting all our emotional eggs in one all-too-human basket.

Although we might wish that these two perspectives would always complement one another rather than be in conflict, Merton's case reminds us that sometimes our task is not to *resolve* conflict but *contain* it. Our attempt to have one side of the conflict triumph over the other once and for all does not bring us peace, but leaves a vital part of our self feeling defeated and our entire life may feel depleted as a result. Merton would have liked to finesse his dilemma by experiencing desire without attachment. But Margie's objections to this solution ring true: to truly and fully desire someone *is* to be attached to them. As Merton found out, desire, in contrast to compassion, is precisely about discrimination, not detachment.

Merton's conflict brings to mind philosopher Isaiah Berlin's insight that some of our most basic values may in fact be incompatible with one another. Berlin says his own unquestioning faith in the unity of the good was first shaken by reading Machiavelli, who championed the classic virtues of the Roman Republic, which valued courage, patriotism, and the capacity to seize and wield power. Machiavelli contrasts these qualities with traditional Christian virtues of "humility, acceptance of suffering, unworldliness, and the hope of rewards in an afterlife. Machiavelli pointed out that these two moralities were incompatible and that there was no overarching criterion by which we could choose between them."

Berlin notes:

The idea that this planted in my mind was the realization, which came as something of a shock, that not all the supreme values pursued by mankind now and in the past were necessarily compatible with one another. It undermined my earlier assumption...that there could be no conflict between true ends, true answers to the central problems of life.

Elsewhere, he said, "What became clear was that values can clash.... Both liberty and equality are among the primary goals pursued by human beings throughout many centuries, but total liberty for wolves is death to the lambs."

Merton might have been able to continue a spiritual life married to Margie, but not the life of a Cistercian monk. Yet even his monastic life was not conflict free. While living a communal monastic life, he longed for the greater solitude of a hermit, and was frustrated by his inability to transfer to another order where that would be possible. At the same time he was the most gregarious of men and deeply engaged with the social and cultural changes of the world around him. His collected correspondence fills volumes.

Because we all want our conflicts resolved and our life to be founded on stable, reliable values, we may be tempted to see in Merton a failure to achieve unity in his personality and his vocation. But perhaps his conflicts reflect instead the capaciousness of his soul, not its flaws. Merton had the courage and honesty to feel many things at once, to be pulled by his conflicting values and desires in opposite directions without being pulled apart.

In the end, Merton remained true to vows and remained in his hermitage. About Margie, little is publicly known beyond the fact that she graduated nursing school, moved out of state, married a doctor, raised a family, and lived happily ever after.

CHAPTER SEVEN

RELATIONSHIPS

I. BEING ALONE

Whether we are sitting alone or together with a group, we are sometimes liable to fall into a way of thinking in which we imagine that our experience is in some way or another unique. It can take many different forms. We might imagine that no one else could be going through the kind of pain we're experiencing, whether emotional or physical. We might imagine that our thoughts, feelings, or the essence of who we really are is intrinsically private—that we fundamentally exist *inside* our mind or our body and that we can only imperfectly send and receive messages out into a world of other separate, isolated minds. Or, we imagine that no one can ever *really* understand what it's like to be me.

What we lose track of in the midst of these various forms of dualistic thinking is the fact that who and what we are is constituted, and constantly, moment-by-moment, re-constituted, by the world we live in and are part of. It's true that I may not be feeling exactly what is going on in your knee at this moment, but I know what pain is. I may not be thinking the exact thought you're thinking at this moment, but I know what thought is. The same goes for longing, anger, anxiety, tension, and so on. All these constitute the emotional ground of what it is to be human just as much as having and recognizing height and weight are part of what it is to be an embodied being. We all share, or rather, are all part of, a common fabric of being.

One of the reasons we maintain some of the traditional elements of Buddhist practice in our lay zendo is that they remind us that whatever we are experiencing on our cushions today has been experienced by many thousands of others, over hundreds and even thousands of years of practice. What we feel, they felt. What we suffer, they suffered. What they learned, we can learn. All of us are simply human beings trying to clarify what it means to be human, and to come to terms with the suffering that being human entails. When we imagine that our experience is unique, we may imagine ourselves particularly talented or particularly hopeless at what we're doing. Sitting may one day catapult us up into heaven; another day plunge us deep into hell. But when we arrive there, we find that heaven and hell are crowded places. Whatever we achieve, others have achieved; whatever we suffer, others have suffered before us. No matter how bad you think you are at this practice, no matter how hard you find it, don't forget: it was designed by and for people just like you.

There's an old saying, "Don't try to put somebody else's head on top of your own." Well, I think we're only tempted to exchange our head for another when we're convinced that its contents are somehow unique—that I could trade my head, which is full of hurt and anger and anxiety, for a different head that has none of those things rattling around inside it. But the more we come to realize the contents of our heads are all alike—that all of us are struggling with the same hurts and problems inherent in being human—the more we're willing to simply work with the head we've got. One's pretty much like another! The strange thing is, it turns out that all those things we thought were so unique about ourselves are precisely what we have most in common.

2. ATTACHMENT AND DETACHMENT

My teacher Joko pretty much summed up her attitude toward relationships in her first book saying, "Relationships don't work." It was a chapter that stirred up a lot of controversy. Rather than talking about everything we normally think that we *gain* from relationships, like love, companionship, security, and family life, she looked at relationship from the perspective of *no gain*. She deliberately focused on all the ways relationships go awry when people entered into them with particular sorts of gaining ideas and expected relationship to function as an antidote to their problems. Antidotes are all versions of "if only..." If only I weren't alone; if only he were more understanding; if only she were more interested in sex; or if only he would stop drinking. For Joko that kind of thinking about relationships meant always externalizing the problem, always assuming that the one thing that's going to change your life is *outside* yourself and in the other person. If only the *other* person would get *his/her* act together, *then* my life would go the way I want it to.

Joko always tried to bring people back to their own fear and insecurity, their own uncertainty. They are ours to practice with, and we can't ask anyone else, including a teacher, to do that work for us. To be in a real relationship, a loving relationship, is simply to be willing to respond and be there for the other person without always calculating what we are going to get out of it. It was a kind of model of selfless responsiveness or giving that defines a certain picture of practice where we just give and give and give.

The problem is that many people come to me and say, "I've been in *lots* of relationships where I give and give and give." But for them it wasn't enlightenment; it was masochism. What they missed in Joko's original account was a good description of what relationships are actually for—what the good part was. So, in addition to being aware of the pitfalls that Joko warned us about, we should also look at all the ways in which relationships provide the enabling conditions for our growth and development. That's particularly obvious with children. We would all agree that children need a certain kind of care and attention and love in order to grow and develop. Nobody would say to a five-year-old, "What do you need mommy for? Deal with your fear on your own!" The thing is that most of us still are struggling with remnants of that child's neediness and fear in the midst of seemingly adult life. Relationships aren't just crutches that allow us to avoid those fears, they also provide the conditions that enable us to develop our capacities so we can handle them in a more mature way.

It's not just a parent-child relationship or a relationship with a lover or a spouse or a partner that does that. The relationship of a student with the teacher, of members of a sangha to one another, to friends, fellow citizens, community members are all factors that help us develop in ways we couldn't on our own. There are some aspects of ourselves that don't develop except under the right circumstances. It would be like being the only person in the world with a fax machine or a telephone. If there's only one of them it doesn't do you much good; they only begin to function when there are others like them.

Aristotle's conception of the virtues provides a way of counterbalancing some of the potential misconceptions that arise in Zen about relationships. For Aristotle, what it meant to become fully human, to flourish and to be happy, was something that he said could only take place within the right kind of communal environment. He is the real origin of the idea "it takes a village" (his word would have been *polis*) to raise a child. He stressed the importance of community and friendship as necessary ingredients for character development. However, you don't find much in Aristotle about the necessity of a partner, or of what we have come to call romantic love, in order to develop. His emphasis was on friendship or *philia,* a Greek word with broader connotations than those conveyed by the English one. For instance, the Greeks took for granted that the friendship between a young man and an older male mentor would often be eroticized. For Aristotle, in order for us to become virtuous, we need as role models the example of other men who have developed their capacities for courage, self-control, wisdom, and justice. We may emphasize different sets of virtues or have different ideas about what counts as the proper behavior for a role model, but Buddhism, like Aristotle, asserts that the basic fact of connectedness and interdependency means none of us at any level can do it all on our own.

Acknowledging this dependency is the first step of real emotional work within relationships. Our ambivalence about our own needs and our dependency gets stirred up in all kinds of relationships, whether it is the relationship that you have to a lover or to a teacher or to an analyst or to your family. We cannot escape our feelings and needs and desires if we are going to be in relationships with others. To be in relationships is to feel our need and vulnerability and dependency in relation to other people who are unpredictable and in circumstances that are intrinsically uncontrollable and unreliable.

We bump up against the fact of change and impermanence as soon as we acknowledge our feelings or needs for others. Basically, we all tend to go in one of two directions as a strategy for coping with that vulnerability. We either go in the direction of control or of autonomy. If we go for control, we may be saying: "If only I can get the other person or my friends or family to treat me the way I want, then I'll be able to feel safe and secure. If only I had a guarantee that they'll give me what I need, then I won't have to face uncertainty." With this strategy, we get invested in the process of control and manipulation of others, and in trying to use people as antidotes to our own anxiety.

With the strategy (or curative fantasy) of autonomy, we go in the opposite direction and try to imagine we don't need anyone. But that strategy inevitably entails repression or dissociation, a denial of feeling. We may imagine that by spiritual practice or perhaps psychotherapy (as we noted in chapter 1, *any* practice or experience can be made to collude with our secret practice) we will get to a place where we won't feel need, sexuality, anger, or dependency. Then we imagine we won't be so tied into the vicissitudes of relationships. We try to squelch our feelings so as not to be vulnerable any more, and we rationalize that dissociation under the lofty and spiritual sounding word "detachment," which ends up carrying a great deal of unacknowledged emotional baggage alongside its original, simpler meaning as the acceptance of impermanence.

We have to get to know and be honest about our particular strategies for dealing with vulnerability, and learn to use our practice to allow ourselves to experience *more* of that vulnerability rather than less of it. To open yourself up to need, to longing, dependency, and reliance on others means opening yourself to the truth that none of us can do this on our own. We really do need each other, just as we needed a father and mother, and we do need a teacher. We really do need all those people in our lives who make us feel so uncertain. Our practice is not about finally getting to a place where we are going to escape all that, but to create a container that allows us to be more and more human, to feel more and more.

If we let ourselves feel more and more, paradoxically, we get less controlling and less reactive. As long as we think we shouldn't feel something, as long as we are afraid of feeling vulnerable, our defenses will kick in to try to get life under control, to manipulate ourselves or other people. But instead of either controlling or sequestering our feelings, we can learn to both contain and feel them fully. That containment allows us to feel vulnerable or hurt without immediately erupting into anger; it allows us to feel neediness without grasping or clinging and trying to hold on to the other person. That means really acknowledging the fact of our dependency.

We learn to keep our relationships and support systems in good repair because we admit to ourselves how much we need them. We take care of others for our own sake as well as theirs. We begin to see that all our relationships are part of a broad spectrum of interconnectedness, and we respect not only the most intimate or most longed for of our relationships, but all the relationships that we have, from the most personal to the most public, which together are always defining who we are and what we need in order to be fully who we are.

Relationships work to open us up to ourselves. But first we have to admit how much we don't want that to happen, because that means opening ourselves to vulnerability and contingency. Only then will we begin the true practice of letting ourselves experience all those feelings of vulnerability that we came to practice to escape.

3. IF IT *IS* BROKE...FIX IT

Acceptance is at the heart of Buddhist practice. We must accept change, interdependency, and vulnerability as synonymous with human life. But how will our life look and feel different if we do accept those things? And what is the difference between truly accepting them and just resigning ourselves to their inevitability?

To answer these questions we must be clear about the basic difference between acceptance and resignation. A quick way to distinguish the two is this: acceptance feels like a starting point, while resignation feels like a stopping point. Acceptance means seeing the facts for what they are and looking forward from there—"what needs to be done *now*?" Resignation means looking at the way things are and feeling hopeless—"there's nothing I can do about it." When we are resigned, we feel overwhelmed and impotent. Problems look insoluble, our abilities and resources feel inadequate to the task at hand, and there seems no point at all in even trying. We are going to be forever a day late and a dollar short, so why bother even starting?

Acceptance puts process ahead of outcomes. It values wholehearted effort rather than preoccupation with result. Who and what we are is defined by the quality of our engagement with this moment, whatever its content. Our lives aren't made meaningful by some score that's going to be tallied up and given to us at the end (bumper-stickers to the contrary, it's not the case that *whoever dies with the most toys, wins*). A sense of value and meaning arises from our responding completely to the moment, with everything at our disposal, holding nothing back, not looking over our shoulder to see if our efforts are being appreciated or making any difference to anyone else.

There's an old maxim, "Do what makes you anxious, not what makes you depressed." When we have to operate outside of our comfort zone, when we have to stretch ourselves to do what's unfamiliar or uncomfortable, when what has worked before isn't working anymore and we are forced to try something new, we may initially respond with anxiety and avoidance. Acceptance means facing and feeling that anxiety and moving ahead anxiously. Acceptance means accepting risk and uncertainty—and that's not going to feel good. How often have I encountered students and therapy clients who act as if acceptance means putting a smiley face on everything? They imagine acceptance is supposed to feel good, that it *means* feeling good about whatever happens. That is simply impossible. When we try it, we just end up denying or repressing all our actual, complicated, ambivalent feelings until they have built up to the point where they can no longer be ignored. Then we are faced with a crisis. Not only do we have to face the problem itself, but our cherished self-image as an accepting person, as a "good" Buddhist, starts to crumble.

Any fantasies of bodhisattvahood that I may harbor while sitting in the zendo crumble pretty quickly when I get home. A roomful of small noisy children—all right, *one* noisy child—can bring out the W.C. Fields in me: I start muttering that the one thing I've learned since becoming a parent is that I don't like children. A student once asked me how much television time I allow my son. I answered, only half joking: "As much as possible—it's the only time I get any reading done."

I have no "enlightened" approach to parenting. As an older parent (my son was born when I was forty-nine) I probably make up in patience for what I've lost in energy. But even that has its limits. My practice is to stay honest, not to stay nice. When I can admit my own irritation and impatience and let myself be less than ideal as a parent, I can realistically begin to sort out how to best handle a complicated situation involving real, complicated people, one only slightly more reasonable than the other. Whenever I find myself getting depressed about how impossible it is to keep the apartment neat and quiet, I have to remind myself to look at my own unrealistic expectations— basically expectations that a kid stop acting like a kid. At the same time, I have to accept I really do prefer quiet to noisy and neat to messy. Acceptance doesn't mean accepting toys and clothes and dishes left lying around the apartment and never picked up. I do have to accept that I'll usually be the one to pick them up, but at least then I'm doing something and not just muttering under my breath.

New students are sometimes surprised to discover I am not a "nice" Buddhist. There's a movie from a while back, *Michael*, in which John Travolta plays an angel with filthy, scruffy feathers and slovenly habits. Someone incredulously asks how he can be that way if he's really an angel. He replies, "I'm not that kind of angel." To anyone who has too many preconceptions about how a Buddhist (and a teacher to boot) ought to behave, I can only say, "I'm not that kind of Buddhist." A lot of that is simply a matter of imagining that even a lay teacher, like me, should look and act like one's fantasy of a monk. A deeper explanation involves how we understand the role of aspiration in our practice. Some practices actively cultivate certain qualities, behaviors, or even feelings. Even if they don't literally try to act "nice," some Buddhists practice loving-kindness meditations or other forms that attempt to directly encourage or bring out our capacity for compassion. It's a big world and that style no doubt has worked for many students over the years, but my own experience with students' secret practices—and with my own—has kept me acutely aware of the potential downside of those approaches. So, even if it's only a matter of a temperament, I'll err on the side of *Michael*.

I teach my students that the main focus of aspiration should always be emotional honesty. I first and foremost want them to be able to acknowledge and experience what they actually think and feel, and not too quickly use practice to try to feel the way they think they *should* feel. Together we try to make explicit their "secret practice," their usually covert attempt to use practice to extirpate or deny some unacceptable aspect of themselves. Practice focuses on staying with the anxiety and anger that mark the boundaries of our comfort zone. If we can work through the vulnerability that lies behind that distress, we will emerge more open and unselfconscious. If we try to prematurely enact a role we think of as more in line with our ideals, our negative emotions will just go underground, only to emerge in insidious and often unacknowledged forms.

Compassion must begin at home. When we are truly able to be ourselves without self-hate or shame, the ways in which we relate to others begins to change. Others no longer have to play their particular role in affirming or shoring up our self-esteem. They no longer have to stay typecast in submissive or self-effacing patterns of relationship out of fear of conflict or risking our anger. As our practice deepens over time, the realization that the self is far more fluid and interconnected with everything and everyone around us opens the door to spontaneous compassionate responsiveness.

Small changes can begin to make big differences. When one person in a workplace begins to act in an open, unselfish way, the whole atmosphere can change. But we must admit that our own expanded consciousness will not by itself raise the minimum wage. There are economic and social injustices deeply embedded in our culture that require our active engagement. There are such things as exploitative jobs, racist and sexist work environments. Acceptance means acknowledging this reality and taking appropriate action.

Our practice can bring us to see that everything is perfect just as it is, but that's no excuse for leaving the dishes unwashed in the sink all night. True acceptance calls forth the appropriate response. When the appropriate response is especially hard and causes us all sorts of anxiety, we may all of a sudden start quoting scripture as a rationalization for our passivity, allowing it to masquerade as acceptance. We try to convince ourselves we are not hurt, not angry, not bored or unfulfilled, and that doing nothing is really our way of practicing with difficulty. It won't wash, at least not forever. When we find ourselves resigned and depressed, all the fine talk about "not fixing" is revealed for what it is.

When it really *is* broke, admit it. Then fix it. Neither psychoanalysis or Zen can't tell you how; their job is simply to keep you honest about what's really going on.

4. A MOTHER'S KISS

Picture a little girl playing in the park—perhaps running and laughing, playing tag with her friends. Suddenly she slips, falls, and scrapes her knee. She starts to cry and runs back to the edge of the park where her mother has been watching. The mother scoops her up in her arms and bends down to kiss her knee, saying, "I'll kiss it and make it better."

This encapsulates something about the essence of practice—though perhaps not in the way one might immediately think. We don't think of sophisticated, rigorous disciplines like psychoanalysis or Zen being like a mother's kiss, but let's look deeper into what's happening here. First consider all the ways the little girl's experience could go wrong. Perhaps she is hurt and when she looks around for her mother she can't find her, and she becomes frightened and cries and cries, unable to console herself. Or perhaps the other children make fun of her and make her feel stupid or clumsy for having fallen. Or perhaps her mother is feeling tired and overwhelmed herself, and when she sees what's happened she gets exasperated and angry, "Now look what you've done!" We can all make up many more examples I'm sure. What they have in common is that the child will come to have certain beliefs about pain and difficulty: "Maybe it's my fault that I got hurt. Is my pain a big deal or nothing at all? Am I being a crybaby? Can I expect help or sympathy, or is the world cruel and uncaring?" Each different version of the story gives rise to its own set of beliefs and expectations.

But what about the first version, when the mother is there and is able to comfort her child and kiss her and make it better? What's really happening? Well, the most important thing to see is that she is, of course, not really making the pain go away with her kiss. What is happening is that she is providing a soothing, containing space in which the little girl can have her experience of pain. The mother conveys both that she knows how much it hurts and reassures the child that the child is going to be OK. The pain becomes normalized; it is nothing terrible or catastrophic, but something that she will feel for a while, and that will gradually fade away—and then she will go back to playing with her friends.

Both therapy and Zen provide something like this container for our experience, one in which we can not only quietly have the emotional experience, but one in which we can watch all the old expectations and fears and beliefs about pain come to the surface. However, one of the other consequences of not having the reliable experience of an appropriately soothing parent in the first place is that we can form magical ideas about what is supposed to make it better. We create fantasies in which someone or something will once and for all make the pain disappear. And we can spend years and years in therapy or in the zendo waiting for that magic to happen, perhaps ending up bitter and disappointed when the magic *doesn't* appear. But nothing ever makes the pain in our lives disappear. Oh, we can create moments of relief or pleasure, but when we think that's the way it's supposed to feel all the time, we fall into one form or another of addiction, desperately using drugs or religion or love as an anodyne. What practice can offer is a container for our pain, one in which the moment-to-moment kiss of attention allows us to experience it for what it is: simply as one part of our ever-changing life.

Just as that little girl needs a trustworthy, secure attachment to her mother in order to develop her own capacity to deal with pain, so as students we need to have a secure, trustworthy relationship with our teacher to learn to deal with the larger pain of our lives. We might say it is a developmental necessity of our spiritual practice just as it is a developmental necessity for the little girl if she is to grow up normally. Although through Buddhist history monks have renounced the security of their homes and family to follow the Way, in doing so they have chosen a form of life that provides them with a clear direction, often a lifelong, supporting community of fellow practitioners, and the guidance of a teacher whom they trust and respect. When we read stories of the lives of old Chinese Zen masters, we read of their intense devotion and commitment to their teachers, with some staying with a teacher for decades, often until the teacher's death, before setting out to teach independently. In the intimacy of dokusan, a student's deepest core beliefs may be shaken to their foundations, but I think it's crucial to remember this is taking place with the secure container of the student-teacher relationship and a deep trust in the rightness of a life of following the Dharma.

This is why the scandals of twentieth-century American Zen have been so traumatic. Not only the teachers themselves, but often the whole community and lifestyle they established were called into question by their misconduct. American Zen communities are all, historically speaking, brand-new experiments. Each reflected the particular teaching style of its founder, incorporating to very different degrees aspects of traditional Asian monasticism.

But it doesn't take a scandal to disrupt a community of practice. The vision of the teacher can change over time, or as the students and community get older, what once felt like an exciting experiment may grow stale. One of my old teachers, Bernie Glassman, has changed his teaching style many times over the years; he founded a Zen community open to both residents and non-residents who continued to work and live outside it; later he shifted his emphasis to work practice and made establishing and running a bakery the focus of his teaching; at another time he emphasized working with the homeless, training them in the bakery, and taking students on street retreats where they lived like the homeless.

Larry Shainberg's memoir *Ambivalent Zen* gives a portrait of this sangha that alternates between being inspiring, funny, and sad. Glassman has gone on to establish the Peacemaker Order and lead retreats at Auschwitz. And in yet another permutation of practice, he disrobed as a monastic and trained as a clown. All of these changes in teaching style could be said to represent his skillful means taking one different form after another, all unselfishly manifesting his Dharma. Yet, no matter how authentic an expression of Bernie's own realization these different forms have been, the question remains for any individual student as to whether or not this form provides the appropriate teaching for oneself. Constant change may free up one student, but unnecessarily and unproductively disrupt the life of another. Not everything a teacher does turns out to be equally skillful and a student's reluctance to undertake—or put up with—the teacher's latest project is not automatically a sign of their recalcitrant egoistic attachments.

Late in her life, Joko decided that two of her Dharma heirs had seriously deviated from the way of practice that she had developed and transmitted to them. Although they were in regular contact over the course of decades of practice, she one day concluded that their paths were progressively diverging and she could no longer accept that they were legitimate teachers. Not only, does it seem, do students require a minimum of constancy from their teachers, but teachers may feel the same need regarding their students, who if they deviate too much from the teacher's way, run the risk of no longer being acknowledged with their lineage.

What kind of constancy can we expect from a teacher? Traditionally, we would say that we should be able to trust that the teacher can act consistently unselfishly or compassionately. What form that takes, however, is an entirely separate question. Compassion can be anything at all that helps a student awaken. One great ancient Chinese master is said to have slammed the door and broken his student's leg, and this action precipitated a great awakening in the student, who would go on to become a great teacher himself. Some teachers believe that constantly undermining student's expectations is the very heart of their teaching. Students shouldn't come to Zen centers looking for security! A teacher's compassion can thus take many constantly shifting forms. We need to acknowledge both the authenticity of diverse teaching styles and just how inappropriate, indeed how harmful, the wrong approach at the wrong time with the wrong student can be. We would like to imagine that an enlightened master is perfectly attuned to each student's individual needs, and varies his teaching style accordingly, but some perfectly authentic teachers are more like one-trick ponies. In the classic koan stories we read of teachers who, regardless of what any student asked, simply raised one finger or even turned away and faced the wall. A thousand years later, we read of the one student, who when treated that way, "got it." But what happened to all the others?

Trust is the absolute basis of the student-teacher relationship. But trust can't forever be blind and a student must balance trust with Buddha's admonition "Be your own lamp."

There's a time to stick it out and practice through difficulty, including what feels like irreconcilable conflicts with a teacher. But there's also a time to cut and run, to admit this approach, this teacher is just not a good fit (and maybe even a toxic one) and move on. Talking to other students and teachers may help you sort out which position you're in. But no one else can decide for you.

CHAPTER EIGHT

WHO, WHAT, AND WHY

I. WHY PRACTICE?

There will always be days, especially when we are getting up early in the morning to meditate, when, in the midst of our sleepiness, we may ask ourselves, "Why am I doing this?" If we are living in the midst of a crisis or some sort of emotional distress, we may feel an urgency to confront or otherwise deal with whatever problem is pressing in on our lives. But if things are going relatively smoothly, if our lives are going the way we want (at least for now) what is our incentive to practice? Is practice on those days simply a kind of maintenance we do to keep things running smoothly? Is it like regular exercise we do to stay in shape or a vitamin we take to stay healthy? To ask why in this way is to assume that practice is a means to an end and that to answer our question we simply need to spell out the benefit we expect to receive from our efforts.

But we can ask "Why?" in many different contexts. For instance, when we ask "Why is the sky blue?" we are asking a different kind of "why" question. When we answer "because molecules of air scatter the shorter wavelength blue light more than the longer wavelength red light," we are converting the why into a how; that is, our answer describes the phenomena at a different level and thereby shows what is happening at an invisible molecular level that gives rise to the large-scale visible phenomenon of a blue sky. But because we can ask "Why?" in such different linguistic contexts, we may get confused about what kind of answer we are looking for.

A classic example might be to ask, "Why is there suffering in life?" All too often, mankind has assumed that the answer must be one that refers to a narrative, purposeful design or intention, usually on the part of a deity who has set the world in motion for reasons of His own that somehow require the existence of suffering in the grand scheme of things. But I would suggest that the only way we can meaningfully answer a question like "Why is there suffering?" is to see it as a "how?" question in disguise, and describe all the ways human beings interact violently and selfishly on personal, social, and political levels. Then we can see where and how we may be able to intervene in particular cases to alleviate some of the pain.

Ultimately, we have to include in our answer something like, "that's the way people are; for better or worse it's always been part of being human to behave like that." When will we put an end to violent and selfish behavior once and for all? Probably around the same time tigers become vegetarians. Their extinction (and ours) is the more likely outcome.

However, we are not *only* violent and selfish animals and we have other capacities we can develop through practice. When we sit zazen another, perhaps a more essential, aspect of what it is to be human manifests itself. When we ask "Why do we practice?"

we are not just asking what we expect to get out of it, we are also asking a descriptive question about who and what we are.

An ancient Zen teacher, Master Unmon, put it this way:

"Look! This world is vast and wide. Why do you put on your priest's robe at the sound of the bell?"

The word "Why" sits at the very center of Unmon's question; what kind of "why" is it? What kind of answer is he looking for?

In this koan, "why" serves as a hinge between two statements: "The world is vast and wide" and "You put on your priest's robe at the sound of the bell." As presented in his question it is as if the first challenges the second. The vastness of the world implies no foundation, no ground—this is the vastness of emptiness—in which nothing has a fixed or permanent or essential nature. Everything is empty, impermanent—why then do we follow the ritual of putting on robes at the sound of the bell?

We are confronted by versions of this why over and over again in our lives and our practice. Students ask, "Life is short! Why am I spending my precious time sitting and facing a wall?" More fundamentally we all ask, "Why do we suffer? Why do we grow old? Why must I die?" What kind of answer are we looking for to questions like these? When Job asked God why he was suffering, God replied, "Where wast thou when I laid the foundations of the earth? Declare, if thou hast understanding."

Job's "Why?" seeks to stand outside of his life and critique it, to suggest that it can and should be other than it is. But God's reply insists that only He can stand outside of life, can shape and judge it. For mortals, there is no place outside of life to stand. So, in our practice, we convert these plaintive questions into simple statements of fact: We do grow old. We do suffer. We do die. Life takes this shape and none other.

For Unmon, putting on a robe at the sound of the bell is simply who we are and what we do. Why does a bishop move diagonally in chess? That's what a bishop is. Though chess—or monkhood—may seem an arbitrary collection of rules, within the game, a bishop is defined by this action. Birds fly, fish swim, bishops move diagonally. Now, of course, I'm not a monk and I don't put on a robe at the sound of the bell. As a lay teacher, the parameters of my behavior are different. There are a lot of different kinds of birds—even flightless birds like penguins. But who I am, what I do, is not a matter of any reason or explanation that answers the question, "Why?" It's simply a description of who I am.

2. WHO'S LISTENING?

Anyone who has ever given a public talk has probably asked themselves the question, "Who is listening?" In our Zen practice however, we ask it about ourselves, not about our audience.

Because our zendo is in the middle of New York City, we rarely are sitting in complete silence. All the sounds of the city—traffic, voices, radios, barking dogs—create a continuous backdrop to our sitting. Sometimes, if we settle deeply into our sitting, we no longer hear anything at all. Most of the time however, it simply comes and goes. It is tempting to treat all that noise as an intrusion and sit longing for a quiet mountain retreat. The other approach is to treat the sounds as a part of our practice, not an obstacle to it. Sometimes I'll tell students, "Be all ears." If we open ourselves to the sounds, we become more and more transparent, the sound passes through us as it passes through the air, meeting little or no resistance.

When we are completely open to the sounds that come and go, we might then ask ourselves, "*Who* is listening to the sounds of the city?"

When we ask "who," our natural reaction is to immediately bring our attention back to ourselves as something apart from the sounds we've been listening to. We often hear talk of "just listening" as if that were a simple, straightforward matter, and I think we all are sometimes too ready to say glibly that we *just sit* or *just listen*. But when we ask *who's* listening, we make explicit the experience of separation that really is going on all the time in most of us, no matter how much Zen talk about "just listening" we may have heard. As we listen, we may be trying to identify the sounds we hear. We may think some are pleasant or unpleasant, shrill or lovely; we may be distracted, entertained, or bored as we listen. Labeling our thoughts allows us to catch all these reactions as they occur, to notice the endless commentary that goes on in our heads as we listen.

As we get experienced in labeling, we get less and less inclined to get caught up in the content of our thoughts, but are able to just watch them go by as thoughts. And the same thing holds true for our bodily reactions, the emotional responses, tensions, and pain we feel as we sit. Gradually we become more willing to let that pain simply be there as part of our experience, the way we let whatever sound that comes through the window simply be there. But it's a long and difficult process. When we listen, we don't think we're listening to *our* sound; but when I'm in pain, it is *my* pain—and it's not so easy to simply sit still and feel it.

The more we allow our inner experiences of thought, emotion, and bodily tension to simply be there, the more they become like the sounds of the city. Some pleasant, some unpleasant—we notice these reactions inevitably arise—but we allow ourselves to feel them as they come and go with less and less resistance or attachment. Inner and outer blur. We simply experience the succession of thought, sound, sensation, and so forth. It's then that we're genuinely just listening, and the question of who's listening drops away.

Practice gets easier over the years, but not because we get good at it. When we start out, practice is something that we choose to do. We try to decide how long to sit and how often and at which center or with which teacher. So many choices! So much effort! But as the years go by, and our practice settles down, it becomes less and less separate from who we are. We make fewer choices; we make less effort, because sitting has become simply a natural expression of who we are. Sometimes I say I'm a very lazy teacher as a way of expressing how little effort it involves. Why do I sit? I simply sit.

Wittgenstein admonished us that explanations in philosophy must eventually come to an end. How do we justify a rule, like the way a bishop moves in chess? It is how the game is played. As Wittgenstein put it, "When I have exhausted the justifications I have reached bedrock, and my spade is turned. Then I am inclined to say, 'this is what I do.'" We are compelled to examine what we imagine would count as an explanation or justification. He goes on, "Philosophy simply puts everything before us, and neither explains nor deduces anything. Since everything lies open to view there is nothing to explain."

Likewise, Zen simply lays our life as it is before us. That life includes suffering, old age, and death. The Heart Sutra tells us there is no old age and death and no end to old age and death. To say no old age and death is precisely to say they have no separate meaning or existence outside of life. They disappear into the vast and wide expanse of life itself. In a strange way, the question of "why" blurs into the question of "who."

Some years ago, my wife Debbie died in a plane crash. When I told my teacher what happened, I said that the one thing I never wanted to hear from her or anybody else is that this had any meaning whatsoever. No unseen plan could justify it. No subsequent good could give it meaning. Death happens. For me, the "why" simply disappears into brute fact. Yet the consequence is that disappearance isn't grim resignation. It is liberation into a simultaneously problematic and problem-free life; it is not a problem to have problems, and problems are no longer separate from the rest of our life.

We have a life of no problems because problems disappear into the fabric of our life, inseparably part of its warp and woof. As part of our Buddhist service we chant, "May we exist like a lotus at home in muddy water." The lotus of enlightenment only blooms amid the nutrient mud of delusion. Yet it is so easy in our practice to become unbalanced, to focus predominantly on either the bloom of the lotus or the messiness of the mud. Either we become infatuated with the flower of enlightenment, forgetting its relationship to the mud of our everyday lives, or we are fixated on our problems, our inadequacies, and doubt anything could ever grow in such muck. We become either connoisseurs of the flower or launch into a water purification project!

I think maybe we need a new American metaphor. Perhaps we should chant, "May we exist like a pig in shit!" The pig is perfectly at home in his shit-world—frolicking, flourishing in what we call waste. We're not so inclined to idealize the pig—to make him an object of veneration or spiritual symbolism like we do with the lotus.... But really the two images are saying the same thing. We have to experience the inseparability of the delusion and enlightenment, not try to eliminate one and stay always attached to the other.

Seeking neither to eliminate delusion nor to find some transcendental liberating truth, we come back to our life as it is. Perhaps only when we forget our aspiration to become Buddhas can we really enjoy our lives as ordinary human beings. Let others decide whether we're acting like a buddha or not. Abandoning self-improvement we exert ourselves fully and naturally as birds who enjoy frolicking in the wind or dolphins playfully leaping in the sea. Or like a pig in shit.

3. THE MEANING OF LIFE

Now that we've addressed who we are and why we do what we do, we might as well tackle "What is the meaning of life?" There's been a lot of confusion about this question over the last couple of thousand years, so I thought I'd take a few pages and clear it all up for you.

Naturally if we're going to answer a question like this, we have to be clear about what it is we're asking. What kind of meaning are we looking for? What exactly does "meaning" mean anyway? Well, as Wittgenstein-Roshi taught us years ago, if you want to understand an abstraction like *meaning*, you shouldn't start off by looking for some comprehensive general definition, but begin by taking a look at the particular instances of how the word is used in ordinary language. So let's take a look at a few of the uses of the word *meaning*.

One use is involved in translation. If we're reading or hearing someone speak a foreign language we don't understand, we may ask what their words mean. And there's a certain analogy to the problem of the meaning of life in this example—often we may feel that life is incomprehensible, we don't understand what's happening to us; we want someone to make sense of it all for us. In the case of translation, we're asking for some correspondence to be established between the foreign words and words in our native tongue. This presupposes we are already familiar with a native language into which to translate the foreign one. But what could be more familiar to us than life? What do we understand better than life that we think life can be explained in terms of?

Another way we talk about meaning is when we ask the meaning of a poem or story or other work of art. Here, sometimes what we're asking for is the intent of the author or artist in making the work. What are we supposed to think or feel or understand from reading it? Western religions have traditionally talked about life this way and spoken of a God or Creator whose intent or plan for our life is what gives it meaning. If you're convinced of the truth of one religion or another, then your question is answered. But if you're not sure which story or faith to believe in, how do you choose? What criteria can you use? Where can you stand that's more certain than the presumed certainty of revealed Truth? A more modern Western approach is to imagine that we are the narrators of our own stories and the meaning of life is nothing more than the story we ourselves choose to tell about it. We can narrate our life as comedy, tragedy, or a heroic quest, whatever form we choose. For some, this narrative freedom seems to convey liberty and infinite possibility, but for others it seems hopelessly arbitrary and unsettled. Again, how do you begin to choose among all the conflicting stories out there? Who's to say if one story is better than another?

Yet another way of talking about meaning is in terms of some function or product. Our life's meaning is found in what we accomplish or leave behind, whether an estate, a work of art, charitable deeds, or our children. But anything left behind is liable to change or disappear or be forgotten. Will the meaning of my life disappear if the book I've written goes out of print fifty years after I've died? Or if the Magid line dies out ten generations from now? Has the meaning of my life retrospectively changed? The ancient Greeks cautioned us not to count a man's life as happy until he's died; some last-minute tragedy, such as Homer tells us befell Priam, the king of Troy, could alter the way we view the arc of his life as a whole.

What all of these example have in common is that in one way or another they locate the meaning of life outside of life— as if the meaning is attached to a particular attribute that can be added to or lacking from life. Often our secret practices contain within them a kernel of our unconscious idiosyncratic explanation for what it is that's going to give meaning to our lives: Happiness. Love. Being free from emotional conflict. Helping others. *If only we could get and never lose this or that quality.*

But our Zen practice (or our analysis) proceeds in an entirely different direction. Here we aim to experience our life from the inside. And from the inside, being our breath, being our body, being just this moment, the meaning of the moment is synonymous with being the moment, regardless of its content.

When we label our thoughts, what we're really doing is practicing experiencing our thoughts as one more aspect of our life that is arising in that moment. Thought has a funny way of trying to step outside of itself, out of the moment, even out of the body, as if it were an independent, disembodied observer and commentator on the passing scene. So over and over we bring our attention back inside. Just sitting. Just thinking. Just being this moment. From the inside, asking the meaning of life is like asking the meaning of a tree or the sky or the ocean. The meaning of a tree is to be tree; the meaning of the sky simply is the sky, and so on. We might say that from this perspective, the meaning of what's happening is inseparable from simply what's happening. And that "what" that's happening moment after moment is all the answer there is. In the end, our question isn't answered so much as it simply drops away.

So next time someone asks you, "What is the Meaning of Life?" you can answer, "Exactly! *WHAT* is the meaning of life!"

CHAPTER NINE

SOMETHING OR NOTHING

I. DOING NOTHING

Wittgenstein said that philosophy leaves everything just as it found it. And in my own way, that's what I've been trying to say about both Zen practice and psychoanalysis. We're not in the zendo or on the couch to perfect ourselves, to become something new or radically different—we're there simply to be who we already are. We practice leaving ourselves alone and just being this moment. Fully being in the moment entails, psychologically, re-owning those parts of ourselves that we've split-off or dissociated from and, spiritually, reconnecting with the whole of life. But leaving everything alone turns out not to be so easy, either in Zen practice or in analysis or, as Wittgenstein taught us, in philosophy either.

Philosophy, almost by definition, is preoccupied with our craving after some form of certainty or knowledge, a desire to find a once-and-for-all basis of understanding the world. That has traditionally led Western philosophers to pursue a *foundation* for knowledge. For something to qualify as a foundation for knowledge, that something must somehow be more solid and less subject to doubt that our ordinary day to day experience, something like a perfect scientific method or a formal logic, something we can fall back on when even our senses deceive us. When Descartes said, *"Cogito ergo sum"* (I think therefore I am), he was proposing just such a foundation—a statement that he said was beyond doubt—upon which he could go on logically, step by step, to create a framework for understanding the entire world. In its own way, the search for foundations is philosophy's attempt to provide us with the same level of certainty that dogmatic religion offers through the revealed word of God—or in Descartes' case, of a way to a secure place for belief in God in the midst of a rigorously logical and deterministic view of the world.

As a young man, Wittgenstein himself started out by trying to define everything that could logically be stated—about everything else, he famously said, we should remain silent. But by the end of his life he came to conclude that there was no place to stand outside of our life, outside our language, outside our ordinary certainty about the existence of the world, cause and effect, and so on, that could provide more logical or philosophical certainty than we already possess. But it took him a lifetime to arrive at that place of leaving everything just as he found it.

In our Zen practice, leaving everything alone isn't such a simple matter either. We might sum up the problem with the single word: the "unconscious." The unconscious is the name we give to all the organizing of experience that goes on behind the scenes of consciousness, outside of our moment-to-moment awareness. Most of the time, we have no idea what our unconscious organizing principles consist of. They disappear into what we call common sense or an unstated view about the world or other people. For instance, we may carry around an unexamined assumption that the world is basically a dangerous place and you must always be on your guard. Or that when something goes wrong, it's probably my fault. Or if only I could find love or become enlightened, my life would be happy once and for all.

So when we think we're just sitting, just paying attention to the moment, nonetheless there are all sorts of ways in which we are subtly shaping our experience into some background narrative or explanation. We can go on for a long time, thinking that we're "just sitting," and still really never dig down into those underlying core beliefs. As I've tried to show, traditional Zen practice can all too easily use the cover of "just sitting" to collude with an unexamined personal "secret practice" grounded in curative fantasy and emotional dissociation. What looks on the surface like a direct or simple engagement with the moment can all too easily fall into a complacent avoidance of our underlying emotional issues.

We may all fall into that complacency in our sitting from time to time, but if we're honest, life is continually offering us reminders to wake up and go deeper. What are those reminders? Anger, anxiety, restlessness, boredom—just to name a few. Each one of these is reminding us that in some way life isn't conforming to one of our underlying expectations. And that's where we have to dig. Anger marks the spot! We have to dig down and find a way to make consciously explicit to ourselves those vague, half-formulated ways of shaping experience that are rubbing up against some inconvenient bit of reality and setting off that emotional reaction. Once we can make them explicit, they become simply one more thought that we can become aware of as it passes through our consciousness. *That old story again.* But until we're really clear and familiar with those old patterns, they'll work busily and continuously in the background, especially during those times when we think we're just sitting, doing nothing.

Real sitting isn't a passive, low-energy drift through the zazen period. Sitting must be alert, active, aware. We should constantly have our antennae out to pick up every sight and sound and feeling that arises in our body. And we have to make that level of attention second nature, like a frog who seems to sit dreamily on his lily pad, but as soon as a fly goes by—ZAP! He wasn't sitting so passively after all.

So: Just sit. Leave everything alone. Do nothing. But really do it.

2. NOT KNOWING

My wife thinks I'm a little nuts about getting places on time. "What difference does it make," she'll ask, "if we're a few minutes late?" From one perspective, of course, that's true, there's usually very little that's actually at stake about being precisely on time. We could even say that one lesson of our practice is that differences don't necessarily make a difference.

The Greek philosophers known collectively as the Skeptics carried this principle to its logical (or illogical) conclusion. Based on the teachings of Pyrrho, this philosophical school taught the practice of balancing every assertion or desire with its opposite, until the mind and the emotions were caught in a kind of stalemate.

The original Skeptics—Pyrrho's followers—flourished in the Hellenistic period (roughly from the death of Alexander the

Great in 323 BCE through the 3rd century AD) Interestingly, Pyrrho himself is said to have accompanied Alexander on his expedition to India and learned his philosophy there. Along with the Stoics and Epicureans, they engaged in a kind of practice that today might be called therapeutic, one aimed at character change and the relief of suffering. The Skeptics were particularly concerned with the sort of suffering that arises from being entangled in beliefs and judgments.

Their technique was to engage any particular belief in a kind of cross-examination, and they practiced showing that, whatever reasons we might have for holding on to a particular belief, there were equally plausible and weighty reasons for believing its opposite. So whenever someone became aware of making a particular judgment, the practice was to look at all the reasons for affirming the opposite judgment as well, so that all judgment came more and more to be seen as just judging—the way we do when we label thoughts. And when they practiced this rigorously, there would come a moment when there would be a complete suspension of all belief and judgment that they called *epoche,* a "not knowing" or pure skepticism. Without judgment, there was just the world of sensation or appearance. Although they actively practiced balancing judgments with their opposites, that critical moment of *epoche* or suspension of belief arrived involuntarily.

The same is true in Zen practice. Realization is not something we can will, it is something that happens to us. It's no good to try and pretend that we can simply suspend our judgments, and be less critical or angry than we actually are. That's a big danger in spiritual practice. We think we're supposed to be compassionate and non-judgmental, so we put on a facade and try to act that way. We indeed can and should control our behavior, but we can't control our feelings, still less our unconscious beliefs. Control may be useful up to a point—it's good to know that we can control our actions and behave well regardless of how we feel inside—but unless we're completely honest about how angry and judgmental we really are, and are willing to sit with those thoughts and feelings and label them carefully over and over, we are never going to engage them in a meaningful way. We can't will the change, we can only be honest, pay attention, and let any change happen as it happens in its own time.

One good student of skepticism is said to have come upon his elderly teacher stuck in ditch and unable to pull himself out. Having learned his lessons well, he knew there could be no conclusive argument for preferring being out of a ditch to being stuck in one, so he just walked on by, ignoring the old man's calls for help! This story is no doubt apocryphal and comes down to us from the historian Diogenes Laertius, in his book on the lives of the ancient philosophers, who probably included it as a kind of *reductio ad absurdum* of a philosophical argument he found ridiculous. Yet there is more than a grain of wisdom in the Skeptics' approach and not a little resemblance to our Buddhist concept of non-attachment. We might hear echoes of the Third Zen Ancestor's reminder that the Way is not difficult for those who do not hold on to likes and dislikes. Knowing, not knowing; liking, disliking; wanting, not wanting—these are the most ordinary, and seemingly inescapable, dichotomies of our everyday life. Yet they are not the bedrock they sometimes appear to be and practices of all kinds, in many different cultures, have tried to loosen their grip on us. Sometimes, what we call common sense can be a cage whose bars we can't even recognize.

When we sit, don't we allow all the usual annoying differences like itches or restlessness or an aching knee not to make any difference to us? Don't we simply keep sitting? This is one way of understanding "oneness." It's an important part of Zen practice not to be buffeted about by our likes and dislikes and sitting still regardless of how we feel physically is the literal, physical embodiment of that lesson. But to an outsider, choosing not to see any difference between sitting all day in near agony and simply getting up to relieve the pain may not look much more ridiculous than saying we don't mind being stuck up to our neck in a muddy pit.

So if I can literally sit still with a painful knee why don't I want to metaphorically sit still for being late?

The answer is that while all things may be equal from one point of view, oneness is not the only point of view that counts. In fact, what we call compassion is our assertion that not all things are equal. Kindness is not equal to cruelty; attention is not equal to indifference; a sink full of dirty dishes is not equal to having them washed and put away.

For me, not paying attention to being on time feels like not bothering to make the bed in the morning—it is a neglectful and disrespectful act—even if the bed itself can't feel a thing and not a soul will be there all day to see if it has been made in the morning or if it has been a rumpled mess until I get back into it at night.

It has been said that art is the replacement of indifference with attention. Nuances that we normally overlook, in shape, color, proportion, and so forth are made the objects of our attention rather than blurring into the background of our perception. Religion could be said to have much the same function, only in religious terms we might say that we replace inattention with reverence. Traditional monastic practice ritualizes every-day life. We extend reverent care to all the ordinary objects of daily life that we encounter and treat them as if they were on an altar, deserving our meticulous if not worshipful attention. Ideally we clean the toilets in the same spirit that we dust the altar and we cook our food and clean our dishes as if they were the most precious things in the world. In his *Instructions to the Cook*, Dogen tells us to treat each grain of rice with the same care we would use to handle our own eyeballs!

Maybe that's overdoing it. Isn't there a point when care becomes compulsion?

I conceded that my wife might have a point about my punctuality when I insisted we arrive at dawn to catch our flight out of Prague. Who knew how long it would take to get out to the airport from the center of town or what bureaucratic red tape we would encounter once we got there? Surely it was only prudent to get there a little earlier than we normally would back home? Giving in to this logic, my wife allowed me to hustle us out of our hotel and out into the dark so early that the airport wasn't even open when we arrived!

Aristotle warned that every virtue, if taken to extremes, becomes a vice. So just as courage can turn into foolhardiness, punctuality can degenerate into compulsivity. Likes and dislikes can become rigid demands and entitlements; accepting everything can be the mask worn by resignation or fearful passivity.

Sadly, there is no rule to tell us when we've crossed the line from one to the other, when we've left the middle way and are drifting toward the extremes. Sometimes we need others to bring us back to the center. When it comes to calling me on my neurotic punctuality—that's my wife's job.

3. NO HELPING

We may come to realize that our practice calls upon us to do nothing—really radically do nothing—and stay with our experience of what is, rather than get caught up in a compulsive cycle of self-improvement. But how are we to respond to the suffering of others? Surely practice doesn't call upon us to do nothing about the suffering we see all around us? What form should our responsibility and responsiveness to others take?

In monasteries around the world, monks since the time of the historical Buddha have chanted four vows that encapsulate the Mahayana Buddhist path. The standard translation of the first vow says, "Sentient beings are numberless, I vow to save them all." What does this mean? What exactly are we vowing to do? What kind of "saving" is this? I'm pretty sure Buddha did not intend this vow to be a commitment to a life of social work, but neither is it meant to be an esoteric admonition that ignores the real needs of real people.

To understand the koan posed by this vow, we must first of all explore in what sense we imagine all beings need saving. We are told that Buddha's own enlightenment manifested in the realization that all beings, just as they are, are already buddhas, whether they know it or not. "Buddhas," by definition, would not seem to be in need of "saving," though we might say that they need to realize their true nature in order to be "saved" from the delusion that they are *not* buddhas. But the words of the Third Ancestor challenge that point of view: "Don't seek the truth, don't even remove delusion," he said.

Buddha-nature is not a potential, it is the way we (and all things, all dharmas) already are. Why then don't we *feel* more like buddhas? The Ancestor might retort, "What did you expect being a buddha to feel like?"

We are all by now familiar with Rinzai's old saying "If you meet the Buddha on the road, kill him." That saying, once startling, is in danger of becoming a cliché, preventing us from experiencing the full force of the words. We need to "kill" any idea we have of the buddhahood being "out there," or down the road or in any way outside ourselves. Yet how many people continue to practice with the implicit goal of someday meeting Buddha? We may imagine we will meet him in the guise of an enlightened master—a qualitatively different order of being than ourselves—or that we will one day, after years and years of hard practice, finally become whatever it is we imagine we want to turn into.

As a child, I read about the wizard Gandalf in J.R.R. Tolkien's *Lord of the Rings*. The portrayal of his wisdom and magical powers no doubt influenced my notions of enlightenment and Zen masters years later. Inevitably all the old stories of our youth, whether taken from Tolkien or the *Mumonkan*, shape our fantasies of transcendence and enlightenment. Perhaps my son's generation will have their fantasies shaped in an analogous way by Dumbledore and Harry Potter. Such figures are the inevitable—and necessary—seeds of our aspiration, yet after they have set us on our way, we eventually have to see them for what they are. The old koans tell stories of people much like ourselves who eventually liberated themselves from their own fantasies of "Buddha." It would be a shame to become so enchanted by their example that we use it simply to renew our own dualistic fantasies of delusion and enlightenment.

We can fall into the same trap with the concept of "saving." To thoroughly "kill the Buddha," we need to confront the paradox inherent in a vow to "save" all those beings who are already buddhas. To make that paradox as vivid as possible, I sometimes have asked my students to consider this alternative to that traditional first vow: "Sentient beings are numberless—to hell with them!"

Zen master Sekito told his students it didn't matter to him whether he was reborn in hell or not. What was the difference between heaven and hell, delusion and enlightenment anyway? Besides, if there are beings who really need saving, where are you more likely to find them than in hell?

But it's we ourselves who really need saving: saving from the idea of saving itself and of ourselves as savers or helpers. We may imagine as Buddhists we should be compassionate, peaceful, kind, helpful—and we should always be devoting all our energies on behalf of others. Well, we don't. Not the way we think we should anyway. But by chanting an idealistic-sounding vow we seem to promise that from now on we'll be compassionate. The problem with this approach to the vow is that it gets us further wedded to the attitude that there is something wrong with us and others that needs fixing. Then we may try to fix ourselves—try to make ourselves "better"—through the practice of helping others. We become enthralled to our own image of ourselves as "helping." We must kill our image of the helper, and of helping, just the way we kill the image of the Buddha on the road. Both sets of images simply further entrench a dualistic way of thinking.

During my training as an analyst, we had a phrase to describe that sort of "help"—the help that inflates the ego of the helper, and keeps the recipient of the so-called help in a forever needy, one-down position: "The helping hand strikes again!" That is why I offer "to hell with them!" as an alternative phrasing. Wipe away all trace of helping, then act. I recall reading about a student who worked with learning disabled children asking Kobun Chino Roshi what the best way was to help them. Her teacher's answer was simple, "No thought of helping."

Dropping the helping hand and any thought of helping can be quite a challenge for anyone who has dedicated her life to one of the "helping professions." But I like to think it is not as contradictory as it sounds. In fact, wherever someone asks me to explain the difference between psychotherapy and psychoanalysis, it's to the whole notion of goal-oriented techniques and to the role of the helper that I try to point. And I like to say the difference is that psychoanalysis doesn't help anybody. Though I admit that may sound a bit facetious, I think it does point to an important distinction. The fundamentally open-ended nature of psychoanalytic inquiry contributes to this stance of "not helping" that I've been referring to. Though patients obviously seek treatment because of problems they want solved, psychoanalysis is not a problem-solving technique. It does not aim at a particular goal or seek a particular outcome.

Despite an increasing trend toward the medicalization of all forms of psychotherapy, driven in large part by the cost containment requirements of the managed care and insurance industries, psychoanalysis by its very nature refuses to be time-limited, symptom-focused, or outcome-oriented. At a time when psychiatry is increasingly being taking over by neurology and psychopharmacology, psychoanalysis continues to define itself in terms of such nonquantifiables as self-esteem, personal meaning, and identity. Its ancestor is not just Hippocrates, who first established the standards for the medical profession, but more importantly Socrates, who led his interlocutors into an open-ended exploration of the nature of the good life.

Being able to leave everything just as it is, is the real challenge of psychoanalysis, just as it is in Zen; a challenge that immediately runs into our resistances, our secret practices, and our unconscious defenses. Norman Fischer, a former Abbott of the San Francisco Zen Center, has emphasized our resistance to leaving everything alone, and the temptation to turn zazen into a technique: "The problem is that we actually are incapable of seeing zazen as useless because our minds cannot accept the fundamental genuineness, the alrightness of our lives. We are actually very resistant to it, we hate it,...we persistently think we need more."

Although both Buddhism and psychoanalysis can be said to share a common goal of relieving suffering, Kodo Sawaki Roshi's admonition that zazen is "useless" should put us on notice that the "relief" being offered may be either indirect at best or, more likely, wholly different from whatever sort of relief we had in mind when we began to practice.

We naturally expect years of meditation to change the *content* of our minds, to transform our personality. Yet, as the example of Sawaki and his student Uchiyama shows, we may remain the sort of person we always were. Years later, Uchiyama (by then Uchiyama Roshi) told biographer Arthur Braverman that Sawaki had been right—after thirty years of practice, "I'm still a wimp!"

CHAPTER TEN

IT'S A MYSTERY TO ME

I. A PILGRIMAGE

A student once said to me that after years of sitting, he knew that his life has been transformed for the better by his practice, but just how it happened wasn't clear at all. "It's a mystery to me," he said.

It's a mystery to me, too.

If it *weren't* a mystery, what would it be? If we could draw a straight line between our sitting for so many hours, in just this posture, in just this setting, and as a result bring about a particular change in our mood or our personality, we would have reduced our practice to a technique. As Stephen Batchelor writes, "A technique is the embodiment of a logical procedure. In employing a technique, we apply a series of interconnected stages, which have been thought out beforehand. Each stage is linked causally to the next. As long as we follow correctly the various stages, we will produce a predictable result.... Any spiritual path that speaks of a series of interconnected stages leading to awakening...has a technological aspect."

We all come to practice looking for techniques that will relieve our suffering. We all come looking for answers to our questions. But though practice can transform our lives, it does not do so by providing us with those techniques or answers we think we need.

Zen doesn't have any answers. Beginning students will often be preoccupied with trying to "answer" koans, not understanding that the questions posed by koans aren't the kind of questions that *have* answers. Instead, koans are stories designed to help us see beyond the dichotomy of questions and answers, to enable us to stay with what seems like an irresolvable paradox, to stay in what seems like a mystery.

One old koan tells the story of a student who asks his teacher for permission to leave the monastery. "Where do you want to go?" the teacher asks. "Around on pilgrimage," replies the student. The teacher presses him, "What is the purpose of a pilgrimage?" After all, doesn't practice teach us that everything we're looking for is already right here? Why travel around looking for it? The student, however, has matured during his years in the monastery, and simply replies, "I don't know." The teacher nods in approval. "Not knowing is most intimate."

Not knowing, intimacy, mystery—all are words that convey a simple, yet profound, openness to the moment without any attempt to master, control, or understand it. Bob Dylan sang, "At dawn my lover comes to me and tells me of her dreams, with no attempt to shovel the glimpse into the ditch of what each one means." I remember writing those lyrics up on the blackboard in a class on dream interpretation at the psychoanalytic institute where I was training. The old Freudian who was teaching the course treated dreams as secret codes that needed to be deciphered and the unconscious as a kind of secret encoder ring that deliberately scrambled the meaning to keep it hidden. Our job was to outwit the patient's unconscious to reveal the hidden message.

Because the analyst was, by definition, an expert at decoding, and the patient, by definition, was determined to avoid hearing the truth about unconscious wishes, whatever interpretation the analyst came up with that confirmed his own theoretical assumptions was presumed to be what the dream was "really" about and any demurral from the patient could be chalked up to resistance.

The prototype of this masterful model of detective work was Freud's treatment of a patient who became known in analytic circles as the "wolf man." That nickname derives from a dream he told Freud he had had as a child. In the dream, he imagined he was looking out his window and saw a tree on the branches of which seven white wolves sat staring at him. By a series of esoteric interpretative maneuvers that one can only learn by being initiated into the secret society of psychoanalysts, Freud unequivocally determined that the dream was a disguised memory of his patient's having witnessed what he called "the primal scene"—that is, his parents having sex. And not only was Freud able to prove that on the night in question the parents had had sex three times, but that they had performed the act in the position he called "*coitus a tergo*"—the father penetrating the mother from the rear, a position that allowed the wolf-baby to have a clear view of their genitals.

I'm not making this up—though Freud, I'm afraid, was. It remains for me a cautionary tale of an explanatory system run amok. Freud was so sure of what he was looking for that he began to see it anywhere and everywhere. Rather than allowing the dream to remain an open-ended metaphor that could be looked at in a number of different ways, the temptation for some analysts is to try to pin down its "real" meaning once and for all. As a corrective to that kind of thinking, a contemporary psychoanalyst, Philip Bromberg, has questioned the very existence of anything we can define as psychoanalytic "technique," if by technique we mean a set of rules of the sort Stephen Batchelor criticized in spiritual practice: "if you do 'this' correctly now, then 'that' will follow later." Instead, Bromberg insists, *unpredictability* is the defining characteristic of the whole process. If that is true for psychoanalysis, how much more so is it true for Zen?

The danger in thinking of psychoanalysis or any kind of therapy as a science lies in the expectation of discovering hidden truths or—worse yet—hidden laws of behavior, if not of existence itself. Unfortunately, religion is not immune to its own brand of this way of thinking. Whenever anyone tries to tell me something had to happen because of fate, or karma, or the Will of God, I hear the same process at work, a certainty in the speaker that his or her belief system has provided him or her with the real, inside story about how the universe works. It's a particular shame when religion, which is so suited to serve as a vessel of mystery, is enlisted instead in the service of certainty. Sometimes I think my role as a Zen teacher comes down to being the one person in the room who says, "I don't know," when everyone else is sure they know what to do—or more often than not, sure they know what somebody else should be doing.

In Jim Harrison's novel *The Road Home,* I came across this aphorism: "Questions are mighty oaks; answers small hard acorns." I'd like to say that I don't know what it means—which is another way of saying I don't want to immediately reduce the image to an underlying meaning or message. I'd like to simply offer a few of my own associations to the images, the way we might approach a dream in a spirit of wonder, rather than investigation: The oak tree stands open to the elements, the rain, the wind, and the sun. The acorn has a vital core, but it is enclosed within a hard shell. Knowing puts a hard shell of explanation and judgment between us and the world. Questions ramify in endless directions; answers bring an end to possibility.

But the oak and the acorn do not exist apart from one another. The mature tree throws off thousands upon thousands of acorns, whose hard shells eventually break down and allow the seed within to grow. Questions naturally lead to answers, which give rise to more questions. To arrest the cycle at any point is death.

We all come to practice with questions, perhaps the most basic of which is "Why am I suffering?" We also come to practice with our private answers to that question, answers that involve blaming ourselves or others, or which catch us in endless cycles of hope and disappointment. These answers lie buried within our minds as grim unconscious beliefs, and within our bodies as hard knots of physical tension. While they lie buried, unexposed to the light and air of our attention, the seed of our vitality is trapped within their hard shells.

We must center our practice not on coming up with new answers to our questions, but on bringing to light the old answers we carry around inside us and which form the hard shell of Self that stands between us and Life. Therapy can help us unravel the history of our answers. Instead of taking our ingrained assumptions for granted, we learn to ask over and over, "Where did I get *that* idea?" Paradoxically, the longer we practice, the less we may be able to answer the basic questions that brought us to practice in the first place. But we are more able to endure their mystery.

2. ANGELS

There's an old saying: "Angels can fly because they take themselves lightly." Even though the word *spiritual* comes from the word for breath, which is nothing but air, too many people seem to make spiritual practice out to be something heavy and portentous, rather than something light. How do we manage to get so mixed up about what to take seriously and what to take lightly?

One way to sort this out might be to say we should take our-*selves* lightly but our practice seriously. Usually, we do it the other way around. We are very serious indeed about ourselves, how we're doing, what we're suffering, what progress we've made, what insight we've gotten or failed to attain. We confuse a practice of awareness with an ongoing, self-conscious monitoring of our own condition. We can become spiritual narcissists, confusing self-involvement with self-awareness. Or we become spiritual hypochondriacs, preoccupied with what we imagine is wrong with our practice. We sit (or even live) as if we constantly have a spiritual thermometer under our tongues (or sometimes, I suppose, up our asses) and a samadhi-cuff attached to our arm that, instead of giving systolic and diastolic ratios, gives a minute by minute enlightenment-to-delusion ratio to tell us how we are doing.

The poet Kenneth Rexroth, who was mentor to the Beat generation of poets like Gary Snyder, Philip Whalen, and Allen Ginsberg, and a pioneer translator of Chinese and Japanese poetry, used to look askance at the earnestness of the first generation of American Zen students. They sat in meditation straining after enlightenment, he complained, like a bunch of constipated old men sitting on the toilet, straining to pass a stool. Or I might say, like a small child in the back seat of a car on a long trip, endlessly asking, "Are we there yet?" One wants to answer, "We're here! We traveled for hours just to see to this particular stretch of empty highway—how do you like it?" "Borrrrrring!" would no doubt be my son's answer—and if they're honest, the answer of a lot of Zen students. Did I really come all this way, for *this?*

Yup. That's both the good news and the bad news: this is it. When we really see that's true, we cannot help but laugh at our old pretensions, our old sense of specialness, our old certainty about the wonders we were going to find at the end of the rainbow. We've spent years facing the wall so that…well, so that we could spend years facing a wall. We haven't gotten anything at all, except we've lost some of our illusions. Maybe dropping all that baggage of expectation has let us lighten up a little about ourselves and our practice. If we manage to drop some of the ballast of "my problems" or "my attainment," and especially that heavy lumpy sack of "enlightenment," maybe the balloon will finally begin to slowly rise into the air, and we can just enjoy the ride and the breeze and the view until the inevitable day when something comes along and punctures our balloon once and for all, and we're dropped on our ass, dead.

Where did you think you were going to end up? In heaven?

3. ROW, ROW, ROW YOUR BOAT

Everyday in our zendo, at the end of sitting, we chant:

Caught in a self-centered dream—only suffering.
Holding to self-centered thoughts—exactly the dream.
Each moment life as it is—the only teacher.
Being just this moment—compassion's way.

I've often wondered how different it would be if, instead, we ended each day by singing,

Row, row, row your boat
Gently down the stream.
Merrily, merrily, merrily, merrily,
Life is but a dream.

In a way, both verses are saying the same thing: life is a dream. But the first presents it as bad news, and our suffering as a consequence of our being caught up in the dream, whereas in the second, we are told, go ahead, enjoy the ride—it's all just a dream.

Maybe, in the first verse, we should imagine ourselves struggling to paddle *upstream,* going against the current, and in the second, allowing ourselves to be carried along by the current, so we don't have to work so hard. The dream is a *self-centered* dream in the first verse, and that is evidently the problem. How? Well, we are both "caught" by our thoughts, not able to get free, and "holding" on to them, not wanting to let go either. Even as we suffer, we are afraid of the alternative, which, even if it means freedom, also means losing control. Who knows where the current is taking us? I'm afraid we know all too well—and we don't like it one bit. What can we do? To whom can we turn for help?

The verse says a teacher is always at hand—that sounds like good news. The bad news is that the teacher is life-as-it-is and that is the *only* teacher. Life as it is means the stream itself. It is always there to remind us that time's arrow flies in one direction only. Our self-centeredness is, at bottom, our desire to stop time in its tracks, to make the water hold still and to stop time itself when we've reached a point in the stream we enjoy or when we're afraid we hear the sound of rapids around the next bend. We are forever torn between trying to hold on and trying to reverse direction. But life is right there as our teacher, showing us over and over that that reversal can't be done. The alternative? Not looking ahead, not looking back, but *being just this moment*. Compassion's way is the way of letting go, of loosening our grip. We've had our teacher by the throat and have been squeezing the life out of her. We can only become compassionate toward our life and toward those around us when we are no longer preoccupied with trying to control the uncontrollable.

Acknowledging the inevitability of change does not mean mere passivity or resignation however. We can still "row, row, row" our boat, but gently rather than frantically. We are honest about what we can control and what we can't, and our efforts are directed toward what's possible, not what's impossible.

Our life is but a dream, self-centered or not. That is, it is something fleeting and insubstantial. All dharmas, Buddha said, share that insubstantiality, that emptiness of any permanent nature. So the usual dichotomy between what's solid and real and what's fleeting and insubstantial dissolves. Waking up only occurs within the larger dream of life. There is nothing more real than our dream to wake up to. The fantasy of a solid, unchanging world or of a transcendent higher spiritual reality are both just part of our dream. Collectively, we have quite an imagination. The things we dream up!

Let's enjoy our dream. It's the only life there is.

NO PATH, NO WISDOM, AND NO GAIN

After three decades of practicing Zen, I think more and more of the line in the Heart Sutra that says that there is "no path, no wisdom, and no gain." I remember when I first realized that these lines seemed to directly contradict the message of the Four Noble Truths, which I had been taught was the basic formulation of the Buddha's teaching. The line immediately preceding this one says that there is "no suffering, and no cause or end of suffering," and then comes "no path, no wisdom, and no gain." The Four Noble Truths on the other hand claim that Buddha realized that life is suffering, that there is a cause and end to suffering and that there is an eightfold path for us to follow, a path that embodied wisdom and the awakened life, a life free of suffering and delusion.

The Four Noble Truths tantalize us with this promise, which is really only a projection of our own fantasy of transcendence. We must pursue this fantasy until we prove to ourselves that it is truly empty. I wish I could say, "until we prove it to ourselves *once and for all*"—but alas, we all seem to need to prove it over and over again, as our fantasy reasserts itself in ever new guises at each turn in our life. Like the mythical monster Hydra that Hercules battled, it grows two new heads every time an old one is cut off. These heads may be named enlightenment, or nirvana, or mental health, or happiness, or nonattachment, or the afterlife. They are literally endless. Hercules finally killed the Hydra by holding a torch to the stump of the head he had just cut off, cauterizing it and thus preventing its regeneration. Perhaps our painful disillusionment with each fantasy in turn can eventually teach us not to allow another to immediately take its place. Yet, how often have I seen students suddenly become enraptured by tales of some new teacher, some new drug, some new technique that promises them the one true answer to all their problems?

If I have learned anything in my three decades of practice, it is that the Dharma is not reducible to any technique or formula. There is no one true way to practice, no single tradition that has exclusive possession of truth, no one teacher who is the unique, authentic embodiment of the Way. When I hear of students or even teachers claiming that theirs is the one authentic way that everyone should follow, I feel as if I were meeting a musician who was telling me that everyone should take up the oboe. A wonderful instrument to be sure—but for everyone?

Just as there is no one instrument that is the sole, true embodiment of music, there is no hierarchy of traditions or practices. Who is to say that the violin is better or worse than the piano? Who is to say that the life of a monk is superior to that of a layperson, whether doctor, painter, or plumber? There may be a greater repertoire available for the piano compared to the harp, but who's to say that a life devoted to the harp is inferior to that of a pianist? What matters is whether we learn to play our instrument well or badly. That's going to take discipline and practice, no matter how or where we do it. Maybe it's not so important which instrument we choose, as long as we can make it *ours*. Likewise, there is no need to stick with an instrument to which we don't feel very suited because we've heard that it's the best or most authentic. Our realization of the Dharma can take place anywhere, at any time, within any form of life, because the Dharma—the basic fact of the impermanence of all things—is constantly manifesting itself everywhere and in everything that changes. You don't have to be a monk to die, or to realize that you're going to. In that sense, we can never master life and death the way we master an instrument. Dying is the easiest thing in the world; everyone can do it. Living is harder—and there is no mastery of life, only clarity about the life that everyone is already living.

When we read the old stories about the old masters who have had great enlightenment experiences, we may come to the rather sad conclusion that only a handful of unique individuals in any generation are capable of having such insights. We read of extreme and seemingly outlandish degrees of effort and dedication, like the second ancestor's cutting off his own arm to prove to Bodhidharma his determination to realize the Way. The extraordinary nature of their lives seems to open up an insurmountable gap between us and them. Is that really what it takes to relieve suffering? If so, the cure sounds as bad as the disease.

What we are trying to come to terms with, after all, is what every human being has to face, the fact of our mortality. Is it really such an extraordinarily rare thing to be able to comprehend the most common thing about our lives? It is as if we lived in a world where only diamonds could be used to put out a fire.

In this alternate universe, fires are easy to start and break out everywhere, but water, which is as common there as here, won't put them out. Only diamonds, which are just as rare as on Earth, will put out a fire. Only a very few unique individuals are capable of finding and mining the precious gems that everyone needs to insure their safety. If suffering is the equivalent of fire in that story, do we really need an experience as rare and hard to acquire and polish as diamonds to deal with it? Or is what we need as common as water—available to everyone who knows where to look?

I don't believe that we live in the spiritual equivalent of that alternate universe. Life and death are not, as they say, rocket science. We can all understand them because we all can, and must, experience them. When we take up meditation or go into therapy, at the most basic level, we are looking for a way to cope with the fact of impermanence, which ultimately comes down to the fact of our mortality. At first, we inevitably try to deny it, control it, or avoid it. Eventually, if we stay with a real practice of emotional honesty and awareness through the failure of one secret practice after another, we may discover the joy that underlies life as it is—this fleeting, ungraspable, uncontrollable life-as-it-is.

We may be scared (to death!) of this truth, and hope and wish and pray for some way out, but we are all capable of eventually seeing our life as it is. If we think that insight is as rare as diamonds, it's because we aren't ready to face what's already right in front of us. If we do have one of one of those rare experiences, what we see is that *everything* is a diamond, everything is revealing right here and now the truth about our life. It's only while we're still trying to escape that reality that we insist there must be a hidden secret that will show us the way out. But it's no secret that there's no way out.

The wisdom of practice is that there is no wisdom—if by wisdom we mean something we can master or something we now know how to do that we didn't know before. On returning from China, Dogen said he had learned that his eyes were horizontal and his nose vertical. Everybody knows it, but almost everybody is deluded into thinking there's something *more* to learn, something hidden and esoteric that is revealed only to a special few. Only after years of searching do we find that there's nothing more to find. Will we be relieved or disappointed?

What is there to gain from practice, after all? We realize that our pain is not a sign that we are broken, simply a sign that we are alive. We aren't broken and we don't need fixing. Everything is the same as when we started.

Let me close this book with a verse I once wrote to close sesshin:

Congratulations everyone!
The Dharma Gate is open and
The Great Way lies beneath our feet
Extending freely in every direction.
Let us enjoy our life together.

NOTES

INTRODUCTION

The *Tao Te Ching* is a 6th century BCE text attributed to Lao-Tzu. A fine English version is available by Stephen Mitchell.

The *Hsin Hsin Ming*, one of the earliest Chinese Zen texts, is a long poem beginning "The Great Way is not difficult...," attributed to the Third Zen Ancestor Sosan (d. 606). The title may be translated as "Faith in Mind" or "Relying on Mind." The full text may be found in *The Roaring Stream* edited by Nelson Foster and Jack Shoemaker.

Bert Lance (b. June 3, 1931) was a close advisor and friend to candidate for President Jimmy Carter, during Carter's successful 1976 campaign.

The question about whether a dog has buddha-nature or not is posed as part of Case 1 of the *Mumonkan*. This can be found in Robert Aitken's *The Gateless Barrier*.

CHAPTER ONE

Why Are We (Really) Meditating?: The *Symposium*, which meant "drinking party," is a dialogue by Plato in which Aristophanes, Socrates, and the other guests each offer their own account of the nature of love. See Plato's *Symposium* in the Waterfield translation.

Three Stages of Practice: Dogen, in the *Genjokoan* section of the *Shobogenzo*, wrote that "to study the Way was to study the self and that to study the self was to forget the self." This translation appears in numerous places, including the translation of the *Shobogenzo* by Nishijima and Cross.

Kiekegaard's discussion of Abraham's exemplary willingness to sacrifice his son Isaac can be found in *Fear and Trembling*.

CHAPTER TWO

Zen and Psychoanalysis: The story of Uchiyama Roshi and his teacher Kodo Sawaki Roshi is taken from Arthur Braverman's *Living and Dying in Zazen*.

What Is the Self?: Heinz Kohut's pioneering work in self psychology can be found in *The Analysis of the Self* and *The Restoration of the Self*.

Hume wrote that by introspection he could only discern one discrete perception after another, never a continuous self behind or in addition to having the particular perception:

"For my part, when I enter most intimately into what I call myself, I always stumble on some particular perception or other, of heat or cold, light or shade, love or hatred, pain or pleasure. I never can catch myself at any time without a perception, and never can observe any thing but the perception. When my perceptions are remov'd for any time, as by sound sleep; so long am I insensible of myself, and may truly be said not to exist." This is from *Treatise on Human Nature.*

Wittgenstein quotes St. Augustine's questions about the nature of time in *Philosophical Investigations.* His discussion of how we use the word "time" and of Socrates' problem can be found in *The Voices of Wittgenstein,* edited by Gordon Baker (pp. 481–87).

Psychologically-Minded Zen: Bodhin Kjolhede, Kapleau's Dharma heir and the Abbot of the Rochester Zen Center, writes about the psychologizing of contemporary Zen practice in the afterword of the thirty-fifth anniversary edition of Kapleau's *Three Pillars of Zen.*

Learning from Problems: Sources cited in this section include: Ford, *Zen Master WHO?;* Bromberg, *Standing in the Spaces;* Downing, *Shoes Outside the Door;* Goldberg, *The Great Failure;* Kornfield, *After the Ecstasy, the Laundry;* Welwood, *Toward a Psychology of Awakening;* Van de Wetering, *Afterzen.*

CHAPTER THREE

Everyday Zen and *Nothing Special* are the titles of two books by my teacher Charlotte Joko Beck.

CHAPTER FOUR

Flypaper: The quote from D.H. Lawrence is from his essay "Morality and the Novel."

The koan in which Zuigan asks Ganto about "the original permanent principle" appears as Case 75 of the *Blue Cliff Record*.

That's Me: "Maybe that sounds better in Pali..." Pali is the language in which Buddha's teachings were first written down; the language he actually spoke is unknown.

Shodo Harada Roshi gives this translation of the Buddha's words on becoming enlightened in *Morning Dewdrops of the Mind*.

You're Perfect...: This case is taken from Michael Wenger's collection *Thirty-Three Fingers* and is reprinted with his permission.

Rinzai's "Buji" Zen: This excerpt is reprinted from *The Book of Rinzai*, with the permission of the translator, Eido Shimano Roshi.

If This Was It: "When Master Mumon speaks..." comes from *The Gateless Barrier*, Case 1.

CHAPTER FIVE

Spiritual versus Material: Hume's arguments regarding the immortality of the soul can be found online at www.anselm .edu/homepage/dbanach/suicide.htm which reproduces the complete 1783 edition of *Essays on Suicide and the Immortality of the Soul*. "Zeno the Stoic said that happiness..." comes from *The Life of Zeno* by Diogenes Laertius, translated by Barry Magid.

Sitting Long Becomes Tiring: Case 17 of *The Blue Cliff Record*, (Cleary, T. trans).

Three Buddhas: This section is based on Case 96 of *The Blue Cliff Record*, "Joshu's Three Pivotal Sayings." I have freely adapted the commentary on Setcho's verses, and I have not hesitated to use the case itself in the service of my own teaching, which some may recognize as deviating in places from the traditional commentaries.

CHAPTER SIX

Asses and Horses: Joshu's dialogue regarding the stone bridge and the wooden bridge can be found in *The Blue Cliff Record,* Case 52.

The quotation "love is the gross exaggeration..." is widely attributed to Shaw, but I have not been able to locate its exact source.

William James initially thought that voluntary poverty and asceticism could serve as the moral equivalent of war. He later amended this idea to include various forms of public service. See Richardson's *In the Maelstrom of American Modernism,* p. 515.

Thomas Merton in Love: All quotes from Merton's private journals are from *Follow the Ecstasy: Thomas Merton, The Hermitage Years.*

The quotes from Isaiah Berlin are taken from *The Crooked Timber of Humanity.*

Paul Hendrickson, in an article in the *Washington Post,* "Trappists: Religion in the Kentucky Wilderness" (Jan 25, 1999), reported that Margie Smith had moved to Ohio, married a doctor, and raised sons.

CHAPTER SEVEN

Attachment and Detachment: Aristotle's discussion of the virtues and the need for community to develop them is developed throughout *The Nichomachean Ethics.*

Hillary Rodham Clinton's book on education was called *It Takes a Village.*

CHAPTER EIGHT

Why Practice?: Unmon's question is from *The Gateless Barrier,* Case 16.

Who's Listening?: The Wittgenstein quotation—"When I have exhausted the justifications I have reached bedrock, and my spade is turned. Then I am inclined to say, 'this is what I do.'"—comes from *Philosophical Investigations* 217.

We are compelled to examine what we imagine would count as an explanation or justification: "Philosophy simply puts everything before us, and neither explains nor deduces anything. Since everything lies open to view there is nothing to explain" is from *Philosophical Investigations* 126.

CHAPTER NINE

Doing Nothing: Wittgenstein said "philosophy leaves everything as it is." This comes from *Philosophical Investigations* 124.

Descartes' search for a secure foundation for philosophy had a personal dimension as well. In his correspondence, he revealed that his mother had died only a few days after his birth and that he himself was a sickly child, not expected to live. He said that he had therefore resolved to make his "happiness depend on myself alone." His famous *cogito ergo sum* can thus be understood as the product of a search for total self-reliance. The psychological roots of Descartes' philosophy are discussed by Stolorow, Atwood, and Orange in *Worlds of Experience*, pp. 1–16.

Not Knowing: The Life of Pyrrho can be found in Diogenes Laertius, *Lives of the Eminent Philosophers.*

Guy Davenport said that "art is always the replacement of indifference with attention." This maxim was printed as a letterpress broadside by Yolla Bolla Press in San Francisco.

Dogen's instructions to the cook about handling each grain of rice as carefully as if it were your own eyes can be found in *From Zen Kitchen to Enlightenment: Refining Your Life.*

No Helping: The Rinzai quotation "if you meet a Buddha…" can be found in *The Book of Rinzai.*

The story about Kobun Roshi is quoted in Sean Murphy's *One Bird, One Stone.*

"The problem is that we actually are incapable of seeing zazen as useless…" This comes from Norman Fischer's *Gethsemani Encounter.*

CHAPTER TEN

A Pilgrimage: Stephen Batchelor's critique of the "technological" in practice can be found in his book *The Faith to Doubt.*

The dialogue about going around on pilgrimage can be found in *The Book of Equanimity,* Case 20.

I've discussed Freud's treatment of the wolf man at length in an essay "Self Psychology Meets the Wolf Man," which is collected in a book of essays on his cases which I edited: *Freud's Case Studies: Self-Psychological Perspectives.*

Philip Bromberg's comment "If you do 'this' correctly now…" comes from his essay "Speak! That I may See You," in *Standing in the Spaces.*

Angels: The saying, "Angels can fly because they take themselves lightly," is often attributed to C.K. Chesterton, though like *"If It Ain't Broke, Don't Fix It,"* it may have an older anonymous or folkloric origin. In my days as letterpress printer, I used it as the motto of my "Dim Gray Bar Press."

Kenneth Rexroth comment—"I do not believe, and never have, in sitting zazen, facing the wall and straining, as at stool, for satori. Satori is an invisible mist, which envelops you unaware, and finally never goes away."—can be found in *Excerpts from a Life.*

Row, Row, Row Your Boat: The chant "caught in a self-centered dream…" is a loose adaptation of the Four Noble Truths that originated at the Zen Center of San Diego under Charlotte Joko Beck.

CONCLUSION

The verse "Congratulations everyone…" was composed to complement another verse traditionally recited at the end of sesshin:

"Attention Everyone! / life and death are of supreme importance/ time passes quickly and with it our only chance/ pay attention to each moment's teaching/ do not squander your life."

GLOSSARY

Definitions taken from *The Shambhala Dictionary of Buddhism and Zen*. Shambhala Dragon Editions. Boston. 1991.

Dharma. Sanskrit, lit. "carrying," "holding." (1) The cosmic law. (2) The teaching of the Buddha.

dharmas. Sanskrit, term for factors of existence, manifestation of reality, phenomena.

Dokusan. Japanese, lit. "go alone to a high one"; meeting of a Zen student with his master in the seclusion of the master's room.

Kensho. Japanese, lit. "seeing one's true nature"; enlightenment.

Mudra. Sanskrit, lit. "seal," "sign"; a bodily posture of symbolic gesture of meditation.

Samadhi. Sanskrit, lit. "establish," "make firm"; collectedness of the mind on a single object through calming of mental activity.

Sesshin. Japanese, lit. "collecting the heart mind"; days of intensive, strict practice of collected mind.

Zazen. Japanese, lit. "sitting absorption"; meditative practice.

Zendo. Japanese, lit. "Zen hall"; where zazen is practiced.

BIBLIOGRAPHY

Aitken, Robert. *The Gateless Barrier: The Wu-men Kuan (Mumonkan)*. New York: North Point Press, 1991.

Aristotle. *The Complete Works*. Translated by J. Barnes. Princeton: Princeton University Press, 1995.

Batchelor, Stephen. *The Faith to Doubt: Glimpses of Buddhist Uncertainty*. Berkeley: Parallax Press, 1990.

Beck, Charlotte Joko. *Everyday Zen: Love and Work*. New York: HarperCollins, 1989.

———. *Nothing Special: Living Zen*. New York: Harper-Collins, 1993.

———. "True Stories About Sitting Meditation." By Donna Rockwell. *Shambhala Sun*. March 2003.

Berlin, Isaiah. *The Crooked Timber of Humanity*. New York: Knopf, 1991.

Bromberg, Philip. *Standing in the Spaces*. Hillsdale, NJ: Analytic Press, 2001.

Braverman, Arthur. *Living and Dying in Zazen*. Trumbull, CT: Weatherhill, 2003.

Cleary, Thomas, trans. *Secrets of the Blue Cliff Record*. Boston: Shambhala, 2000.

Clinton, Hillary Rodham. *It Takes a Village*. New York: Simon and Schuster, 1996.

Dogen, Eihei and Kosho Uchiyama. *From Zen Kitchen to Enlightenment: Refining Your Life*. Translated by Tom Wright. Trumbull, CT: Weatherhill, 1983.

Downing, Michael. *Shoes Outside the Door*. San Francisco: Counterpoint, 2001.

Fischer, Norman. "On *Zazen*." In *The Gethsemani Encounter: A Dialogue on the Spiritual Life by Buddhist and Christian Monastics*, 41–45. Edited by Donald W. Mitchell and James A. Wiseman. New York: Continuum, 1999.

Ford, James Ishmael. *Zen Master Who?: A Guide to the People and Stories of Zen*. Boston: Wisdom Publications, 2006.

Foster, Nelson and Jack Shoemaker, eds. *The Roaring Stream*. Hopewell, NJ: Ecco, 1996.

Goldberg, Natalie. *The Great Failure: My Unexpected Path to Truth*. San Francisco: HarperCollins, 2005.

Griffin, John Howard. *Follow the Ecstasy: Thomas Merton, the Hermitage Years, 1965–1968*. Forth Worth, TX: Latitudes Press, 1983.

Harada, Shodo. *Morning Dewdrops of the Mind: Teachings of a Contemporary Zen Master*. Berkeley: Frog, 1993.

Hume, David. *A Treatise on Human Nature*. 2nd ed. Analytical index by L.A. Selby-Bigge. Edited by P.H. Nidditch. Oxford: Oxford University Press, 1978.

———. *Essays on Suicide and the Immortality of the Soul*. Whitefish, MT: Kessinger Publishing, 2004.

Kapleau, Philip. *The Three Pillars of Zen*. 35th anniv. ed. New York: Anchor Books, 2000.

Kierkegaard. *Fear and Trembling*. Edited by C. Stephen Evans and Sylvia Walsh. Cambridge: Cambridge University Press, 2006.

Kohut, Heinz. *The Analysis of the Self: A Systemic Approach to the Psychoanalytic Treatment of Narcissistic Personality Disorder*. 11th ed. Madison, CT: International Universities Press, 1971.

———. *The Restoration of the Self*. Madison, CT: International Universities Press, 1976.

Kornfield, Jack. *After the Ecstasy, the Laundry: How the Heart Grows Wise on the Spiritual Path*. New York: Bantum Books, 2000.

Laertius, Diogenes. *The Lives of the Eminent Philosophers*. Translated by R.D. Hicks. 2 vols. Cambridge: Harvard University, Loeb Classical Library Press, 1925.

———. *The Life of Zeno*. Translated by Barry Magid. Frankfurt, KY: Larkspur Press, 1996.

Lawrence, D.H. "*Morality and the Novel*," in: *Study of Thomas Hardy and Other Essays*, Cambridge: Cambridge University Press, 1985.

Lao Tzu. *Tao Te Ching*. Translated by Stephen Mitchell. New York: HarperCollins, 1988.

Magid, Barry, ed. *Freud's Case Studies: Self-Psychological Perspectives*. Hillsdale, NJ: Analytic Press, 1993.

Murphy, Sean. *One Bird, One Stone: 108 American Zen Stories*. New York: St. Martin's Press, 2002.

Nishijima, Gudo and Chodo Cross, trans. *Master Dogen's Shobogenzo*. Woods Hole, MA: 1998.

Plato. *Symposium*. Translated by Robin Waterfield. Oxford: Oxford University Press, 1994.

Rexroth, Kenneth. *Excerpts from a Life*. Santa Barbara, CA: Conjunctions, 1981.

Richardson, Robert D. *William James: In the Maelstrom of American Modernism*. New York: Houghton Mifflin, 2006.

Rinzai. *The Book of Rinzai*. Translated by Eido Shimano. New York: Zen Studies Society Press, 2005.

Shainberg, Lawrence. *Ambivalent Zen*. New York: Pantheon, 1995.

Stolorow, Robert, George E. Atwood, and Donna M. Orange. *Worlds of Experience: Interweaving Philosophical and Clinical Dimensions in Psychoanalysis*. New York: Basic Books, 2002.

Van de Wetering, Janwillem. *Afterzen: Experiences of a Zen Student Out on His Ear*. New York: St. Martin's Press, 1999.

Welwood, John. *Toward a Psychology of Awakening: Buddhism, Psychotherapy, and the Path of Personal and Spiritual Transformation*. Boston: Shambhala, 2000.

Wenger, Michael. *Thirty-Three Fingers: A Collection of Modern American Koans*. San Francisco: Clear Glass, 1994.

Wick, Gerry Shishin. *The Book of Equanimity: Illuminating Classic Zen Koans*. Boston: Wisdom Publications, 2005.

Wittgenstein, Ludwig. *Philosophical Investigations*. Translated by G.E.M. Anscombe. London: Basil Blackwell, 1953.

Wittgenstein, Ludwig and Friedrich Waismann. *The Voices of Wittgenstein: The Vienna Circle*. Edited by Gordon Baker. London: Routledge, 2003.

INDEX

ABOUT THE AUTHOR

Barry Magid is a psychiatrist and psychoanalyst in New York City. He received his M.D. from the New Jersey College of Medicine in 1975, and completed his psychoanalytic training at the Postgraduate Center for Mental Health in 1981. He is a currently a faculty member and supervisor at that Institute, as well as at the Institute for Contemporary Psychotherapy in New York. He has published numerous articles within the psychoanalytic field of Self Psychology and is the editor of *Freud's Case Studies: Self Psychological Perspectives,* and the author of *Ordinary Mind: Exploring the Common Ground of Zen and Psychotherapy.*

In October 1996, Charlotte Joko Beck gave him permission to establish The Ordinary Mind Zendo as an affiliate of the San Diego Zen Center, and to serve as its teacher. He received Dharma Transmission from her in1999. He is committed to the ongoing integration of the practices of psychodynamic psychotherapy and Zen.

Since 1989, he has also handprinted books at the Center for Books Arts in New York City, and published limited editions of works by Wendell Berry, Guy Davenport, Mark Doty, Jonathan Greene, Jim Harrison, James Laughlin Thomas Merton, Robert

Stone, Charles Tomlinson, Jonathan Williams, William Carlos Williams and others under the imprint of the Dim Gray Bar Press. His own translation of *Diogenes Laertius,* "Life of Zeno," was published by Larkspur Press in 1996.

Also Available from Wisdom Publications

Saying Yes to Life (Even the Hard Parts)
Ezra Bayda with Josh Bartok
Foreword by Thomas Moore
264 pages, ISBN 0-86171-274-9, $15.00

"Ezra Bayda is one of our favorite Buddhist teachers. In this astonishing collection of sayings and short meditations, he delivers profound Buddhist wisdom laced with simplicity, practicality, depth, and inspirational vitality."—*Spirituality and Health*

"This book is full of many small gems of wisdom and insight. If even one of these encourages you to shift your habitual way of thinking and behaving, you will be highly rewarded."— Gerry Shishin Wick, Roshi, author of *The Great Heart Way*

Zen Meditation in Plain English
John Daishin Buksbazen
Foreword by Peter Matthiessen
128 pages, ISBN 0-86171-316-8, $12.95

"Buksbazen, a psychotherapist and Zen priest, offers practical and down-to-earth advice about the specifics of Zen meditation: how to position the body; how and when to breathe; what to think about. Helpful diagrams illustrate the positions, and Buksbazen even provides a checklist to help beginners remember all of the steps. He builds a strong case for the powerful effect of being involved with a community of other practitioners and follows this with concrete information about group practice, including meditation retreats and other intensive training periods. This is a fine introduction to Zen meditation practice, grounded in tradition yet adapted to contemporary life."—*Publishers Weekly*

Mindful Therapy
A Guide for Therapists and Helping Professionals
Thomas Bien, Ph.D.
304 pages, ISBN 0-86171-292-7, $17.95

"This is the voice of a wise and sincere practitioner of the twin paths of emotional healing—mindfulness and psychotherapy. Bien explains the core ideas of Buddhist psychology in language that is likely to make sense to beginners and seasoned practitioners alike, and he provides a wealth of insights and techniques to make the teachings more accessible to clients. A rich, timely contribution."—Christopher K. Germer, PhD, Harvard Medical School, and co-editor, *Mindfulness and Psychotherapy*

On Zen Practice
Body, Breath, and Mind
Edited by Taizan Maezumi Roshi and Bernie Glassman
Foreword by Robert Aitken
208 pages, ISBN 0-86171-315-x, paper, $16.95

This updated landmark volume makes available for the first time in decades the teachings that were formative to a whole generation of American Zen teachers and students. Conceived as the essential Zen primer, *OZP* addresses every aspect of practice: beginning practice, chanting, *sesshin*, *shikantaza*, working with Mu, the nature of koans, and more. The contributors here are some of modern Zen's foremost teachers, largely responsible for Zen's steady growth in America. This newly refined volume is an unmatched teaching and reference tool for today's Zen practitioner.

Ordinary Mind
Exploring the Common Ground of Zen and Psychoanalysis
Barry Magid
Foreword by Charlotte Joko Beck
224 pages, ISBN 0-86171-495-4, $15.95

"Magid's book has a broad appeal; many people will find something useful here. [. . .] A valuable step forward in making two radically different healing techniques available to each other in both thought and practice. With the help of this book, teachers and students in both camps reflect fruitfully on the benefits of the other."—*Psychologist-Psychoanalyst*

Psychoanalysis and Buddhism
An Unfolding Dialogue
Edited by Jeremy D. Safran
464 pages, ISBN 0-86171-342-7, $19.95

"An extraordinary book. While Jack Engler's brilliant opening essay sets the bar high for the other contributors, the entire volume is full of wonderful surprises. This is a beautifully conceived work: innovative, provocative, fascinating and useful. Jeremy Safran deserves much praise."—Mark Epstein, M.D., author of *Thoughts without a Thinker*